THERE LIES A FAIR LAND:
AN ANTHOLOGY OF NORWEGIAN-AMERICAN WRITING

THERE LIES A FAIR LAND
An Anthology of
Norwegian-American Writing

edited by
John Solensten

with graphics by
Arch Leean

Many Minnesotas Project #1
New Rivers Press
1985

Some of this material has appeared in other publications. Our thanks to the editors. This material is listed on page 176 of this volume.

Publication of *There Lies a Fair Land* has been partially supported by grants from the Northwest Area Foundation, Norwest Banks, the Arts Development Fund of the United Arts Council, and the First Bank System Foundation.

New Rivers Press books are distributed by

Bookslinger	and	Small Press Distribution
213 E. 4th St.		1784 Shattuck Ave.
St. Paul, MN		Berkeley, CA
55104		94709

There Lies a Fair Land has been manufactured in the United States of America for New Rivers Press, Inc. (C. W. Truesdale, editor/publisher), 1602 Selby Ave., St. Paul, MN 55104 in a first edition of 2000 copies.

For Brenda Ueland,
(1891-1985)

THERE LIES A FAIR LAND:
AN ANTHOLOGY OF NORWEGIAN-AMERICAN WRITING

IV: GOING BACK:
THE LAND AND THE MEMORY

INTRODUCTION

On the Fourth of July, 1825, the *Restoration*, a 39-ton sloop with about 50 passengers aboard, sailed out of Stavanger harbor. Some of the passengers were crying as they waved farewell; most were looking out to sea—hope and fear and determination on their faces. Their motives for leaving their homeland typified the motives of those who would later take passage to America. They were Quakers or Quaker sympathizers who had experienced discrimination in Lutheran Norway; they were also practical people fleeing bad economic conditions in Norway. The men, especially, had the "fever"—the "America fever"—a dis-ease condemned later on from Lutheran pulpits when thousands of good Lutheran parishioners caught it and it began to assume epidemic proportions. The passengers on the *Restoration*, were generally poor people. They found cheap passage on the *Restoration*, a crazy old ship in such poor condition that its captain was arrested in New York for subjecting his passengers to such danger.

The *Restoration* carried with it not only its passengers but also motifs that were to dominate the story of subsequent immigration: the romanticism of the restless quest; the perils and harsh realities of passage; the Reformation tradition of revolt against authority and seeking a freer or purer community of worship in a New Land; a mixture of motives that were both practical and idealistic; a deep sense of uprooting from the security—moral and physical—of communal life close to the land in the Old Country; a collective sense of the need to establish new communities of kindred spirits in the New World.

It seemed logical to begin this section with O.E. Rolvaag's portrait of Kleng, Pierson (variously spelled Kleng or Cleng and Peerson or Pierson) whose monument in the cemetary at Norse, Texas reads:

Kleng Peerson
The First Norwegian Immigrant to America
Came to America in 1821
Born in Norway, May 17, 1782
Died in Texas, December 16, 1865
Grateful Countrymen in Texas Erected
This Monument to His Memory

Pierson, who met the Quakers group aboard the *Restoration* in New York and helped them settle at Kendall in that state, has become legendary in the Norwegian immigrant experience—the archetypal land-finder and "westerner"—an unselfish and restless spirit who crossed the Atlantic several times, tramped thousand of miles over prairie and wilderness and inspired thousands of his countrymen to follow him.

By 1925, when the Norse-American Centennial celebration was held in June at the Minnesota State Fair Grounds, approximately one million Norwegians had immigrated to America. In Europe, only Ireland had sent a larger proportion of her population to the New Land.

—John Solensten
St. Paul, Minnesota 1985

I. LAND-SEEKING AND SETTLING

CLENG PIERSON

O. E. Rölvaag

BOTH MEN AND women felt the sheer loneliness of farm life on the American plains. Deprived of social contact with others and tied to the desperate hardship of a narrow world, some went insane; many wasted away and perished before their time. Sometimes religious conviction became an obsession. In O. E. Rolvaag's Giants In The Earth *Beret Hansa begins to perceive the prairie as a moral desert. When she learns that her husband has burned homestead stakes driven into the land by Irish settlers who had arrived earlier, she perceives the burning of the stakes as a symbol of the loss of morality which she feels has accompanied their abandonment of their Norwegian homeland.*

The perils of settling on remote reaches of the prairie were manifold in immigrant literature. They are also reflected in earlier American literature and folklore from James Fenimore Cooper's Leatherstocking Tales to the Pike County ballads. The frontier, as Frederick Jackson Turner has suggested, has always been a meeting place between civilization and savagery—a meeting place where only the laws of nature prevailed or where men might make their own law—if only until the sheriff and the schoolteachers arrived. Meanwhile—out on the edges of settlement—men acted out little dramas of desperate loneliness and death and sometimes their own brand of vengeance.

Let me tell you a story.

Ninety-six years ago Cleng Pierson, the pathfinder of Norwegian immigration to America, started out on foot from the shore of Lake Ontario in the State of New York to hunt for a suitable location for a Norwegian colony. Eight years previous, on the shores of that lake, he had located the first band of Norwegians in America. But the soil there was sandy and, besides, hard to clear; and, little by little, Cleng Pierson came to realize that this place was no Promised Land.

In the summer of 1833 we find him on the trail to Sunset Land. He is walking, and alone. One fine day he trudges into the city of Chicago. Chicago in 1833 —a few scattered huts and shanties. The magnificence of the great metropolis of

13

the Mississippi Valley didn't impress him. In fact, he looked at the place with disdainful eyes.

Not far away a great body of water lay beckoning. Cleng Pierson had been a sailor before he came to America. No wonder that sight of Lake Michigan's clear water cast its spell upon him. Walking down to the shore, he began to follow it northward. One evening toward sundown he strolled into the great city of Milwaukee. Nothing imposing to greet his eye here, either. The place had only three houses, one of which stood empty; the other two were occupied by the Juneau brothers. "What will I find if I continue northward from here?" Cleng Pierson asked. "Nothing but woods from here to the end of the world," was the answer.

Cleng Pierson left southern Wisconsin, a greatly disappointed man. Would he never find the Promised Land? Where was he to look for it? From Milwaukee he struck out south and in a westerly direction, over the low, wide-bosomed prairies of northern Illinois. Of roads there was not even a trace. For days he walked, his eye spying and searching, like some lonely sea gull crossing an ocean.

No human habitation anywhere, not even a wigwam. Picture to yourself this solitary figure plodding on! The tall grass of the prairie lands tires his feet; the rays of the hot sun seem to seek him out; at times a crashing thunderstorm punctures the strange silence. What is he thinking of as he sits there at night, alone by his camp fire? What does he want in this alien wilderness? The man must be mad beyond redemption! Not the faintest inkling did he have of the history he was making. Men thus singled out by Destiny of some great purpose seldom do have.

Often, later in life, Cleng Pierson stated that this was the worst trip he ever made, though he made many arduous ones. Late one evening, after weeks of tramping, he trudged into a country that seemed different. Was it only the twilight that was fooling him? For several days he had had no food to speak of. Utterly exhausted, he flung himself down by a tree and fell asleep.

There is a story; it is beautiful, and I like to tell it. As he lay there that night under the starlit sky he had a vision: In his dream he saw a picture—a whole settlement, well built up . . . fine dwellings . . . red-painted barns . . . waving fields of golden grain. Close by him he saw a church, from which he heard clearly the old, stately hymns sung in the churches of Norway.

So far the legend. When he awoke in the morning, the pleasantest sight that had ever struck his eye greeted him. The endless reaches of flat, low prairie were gone; instead had come to a gently rolling country; it seemed to lie high; in several places grew thickets of tress, natural groves for shelter. He found creeks, too. To the westward he came upon a river, the banks of which were richly wooded. The place where he now stood surveying the new Kingdom is about one quarter of a mile southwest of the little town of Norway in La Salle County, Illinois.

One fine day late in the fall of the same year Cleng Pierson came walking back to the little colony on Lake Ontario. The story he told was so marvelous that by far the greater number concluded to pull up stakes and move to Illinois. This they did the following summer, and thus it happened that the first colony of Norwegians was established in the Middle West. Many others were to follow.

Cleng Pierson's journey in the summer of 1833 is of importance not only to American history; in the history of Norway during the nineteenth century it cuts a far bigger swatch, for no other country, with the exception of Ireland, has, in proportion to its population, given America so many citizens. Had not this man discovered the Middle West for the Norwegians, emigration from that country would presumably have been light. But after moving to Illinois, the colony in La Salle County could write back a glowing account of the new Goshen. And the result was soon to be felt—there are now as many American citizens of Norwegian descent as there are people in Norway.

A FUNERAL IN PIONEER TIMES

Ole A. Buslett

ACCORDING TO DR. NEIL T. ECKSTEIN, "A Funeral in Pioneer Times" is a part of a frontier oral tradition in storytelling and passed from one storyteller to another with minor changes. This is Ole Buslett's version of the tale, which O. E. Rölvaag included in a 1918 collection of representative writings depicting the immigrant experience.

"Piskopalen" in the story is a Swedish Episcopalian minister. Old Ingebret, the "inside narrator," confuses "ordination" and "organization" and punctuates his telling with "Tvi!"—a squirt of tobacco juice. A "klokker" was a bell-ringer, hymn leader and Amen repeater in immigrant churches. Whisky was cheap and life hard. That may help to explain (but to pietists never justify) the heavy drinking on such an occasion.

Ingebret Tveitan from Slemdal had a remarkable memory and was a good storyteller. He could tell many stories from the times of the first Norwegian settlers in Wisconsin, and when he came to an important point in the story, he would punctuate it by spitting.

"I have been at a good many of the gatherings in the early settlements," Old Ingebret said,—"I have been at weddings, funerals, Christmas parties, and many other kinds of parties. You can just bet that they were often lively, with dancing and other kinds of fun. And we always had a little whisky because it was cheap in those days and cost only 20 cents a gallon. Tvi! During some funerals we had almost as much fun as at a wedding. On the day of the funeral they conducted the service with proper weeping and sorrow and songs, but in the evening it sometimes happened that the whole funeral procession would gather at the house of mourning and sing songs, drink whisky, and play cards. We would also tell tales and other stories and sometimes carry on this way until morning. Ja, I have heard about a 'Klokker' who was so crazy about card playing that he would pack up his playing cards in one pocket and his hymn book in the other whenever there was a funeral. *Fy*, that was downright heathendom! Tvi!"

16

"But there's an old proverb that says that folks scarcely get something into their skulls before their hair bristles. But when we are old and gray, we begin to get a little common sense, they say. Tvi!"

Old Ingebret bit off another "chaw" and took up his story again—"As I was saying, I have been along with many of these celebrations, both here in America and in the Old Country. But in the settlement where I first lived in this country, I was at a funeral, the likes of which I have never seen before or after, that is for sure! Tvi!"

"At that time there lived a strange fellow in our neighborhood by the name of Kristen Puttekaasen—a good fellow who wouldn't harm a flea, good for work and good for drinking whisky. One could say the same about him as the man said about his mare, 'She's good at pulling, but she's also mighty good at eating.' This Kristen believed that liquor was good for everything, and, of course, he wasn't the only one with that belief. On a crackling cold day in the winter, a snort was especially good, he said, because it warmed and invigorated both body and soul. Also on a roasting hot summer day, it was especially good because it cooled a fellow off so wonderfully well, he said. Tvi!"

"There was a boy by the name of Ola, if I remember correctly, who was a nephew to Puttekaasen and made his home with him. This boy took sick and died, and Kristen wanted to give him a proper burial. It was so curious and strange, Kristen said, that Ola, who was such a stout and strong and healthy lad, should be so short-lived. There are a good many other young fellows who are not as healthy as Ola was. Some of these others had the same sickness, but they managed to scrape through. Well, that's the way it goes—some stand and some fall. But Ola was such an unusually good boy. He is my own blood relation, and he shall have a proper Christian burial. I have arranged both for the preacher and for the liquor for the funeral. And I think that Ola Haugen, the Klokker, can sing him to the grave, he said. Tvi!"

"In those days there were no 'organized' preachers. Well, maybe Ditriksen had come to Kaskeland. He was 'organized' properly in Norway, but he had not come our way yet. But there was a Swedish lay-preacher that the 'Piskopalen' had 'organized.' The Norwegians sometimes called him 'Piskopalen' and sometimes the Swedish preacher. He was the one who should 'serve' for Ola's burial. Tvi!"

"Some of the older Norwegians who remembered the Swedish war and were angry with the Swedes thought that a Swede should not have the funeral sermon for a Norwegian. That the preacher was 'Piskopalen' was bad enough, but it was much worse that he was a Swede. But some of the others didn't see it this way, and Puttekaasen was saying about the same thing that Pastor Ottesen of Kaskeland once said—'Any blockhead can become a preacher'—he said. He really did say that! Tvi!"

"So the funeral day came and the funeral liquor came, and the whole neighborhood came with their 'horned horses' (oxen), for other horses were not to be found in the entire settlement, as far as I know."

"The Swedish preacher told that the Canal Lands would soon come on the market. A company had received a land grant from the government to build a canal—I believe that it was between Rock River and Fox Lake, if I remember right. Many Norwegian and Swedish families had settled upon these lands which were called Canal Lands. But the Canal came to nothing, and so the lands were to be put up for sale. Right after the funeral the Swedish preacher was planning to go to Milwaukee, and so he promised these folks who had settled on the Canal Lands that he would find out if the lands would soon be for sale."

"While the Swedish preacher and the others stood and talked about the Canal Lands, Puttekaasen had been preparing a suitable punch for serving during the funeral. Tvi!"

"And so he went up to 'Piskopalen' and said, 'Herr Pastor! We Norwegians are used to taking a little drink before we begin this kind of business."

"'Yes, we must follow your custom,' said the pastor."

"'Skaal, Herr Pastor!' Puttekaasen said, and drank to his health."

"'Thank you very much, but I will not imbibe,' the 'Piskopalen' said."

"So they sang a hymn and 'Piskopalen' had a sermon, which really wasn't so bad. Jakob Rosholdt should carry the coffin because he had the best oxen and the best sled in the neighborhood. 'Piskopalen' and Puttekaasen took their places in one of the rear sleds. The procession was about to start when Puttekaasen yelled out at the top of his lungs, 'Whoa! Stop, Jakob! Don't be in such a terrible hurry. We must have a drink for the road.' And so he turned to 'Piskopalen' and said: 'Herr Pastor! We Norwegians are used to taking a good bracer before we start out! Tvi!"

"'We will follow your custom,' said 'Piskopalen.'"

"So Puttekaasen went up to Jakob, who was driving in the front, and treated him first, and then worked his way back to the others. There must have been six or seven teams of oxen, I suppose, and finally the procession got underway. But when we had come about halfway, we saw Puttekaasen running and stirring up a cloud of snow. He ran up forward to Jakob and yelled, 'Whoa! Whoa! Stop! We must have a drink now on the road!' Tvi!"

"And so he ran in a great hurry to the Swedish preacher and said, 'Herr Pastor! We Norwegians have a custom of taking a snort on the road also.'"

"'We will follow your custom,'' said 'Piskopalen' again."

"When they all had their drinks, they drove on again, and finally they came to the cemetery. Tvi!"

"But this was not the end of it because Puttekaasen had more in his jug, and so he went up to 'Piskopalen' and said, 'Herr Pastor! We Norwegians have the custom of taking a swig before we begin this business.'"

"'We will follow your custom,' said the Swede."

"When we had the last drop out of the jug, we had to let down the coffin, but it happened that two of the least steady fellows fell into the grave before the coffin was in place. But now the coffin came down anyway and was standing on end for a while. We had to haul it up again, and then we finally got it set down properly, and the preacher conducted the commital and had a short prayer. The Klokker and Puttekaasen, who stood next to the preacher, joined in singing very loudly, 'Hvo vet hvor naer mig er min ende' (Who knows how near is the end). When they had come to the middle of the verse, Puttekaasen said, 'Herr Pastor! You must remember to see how it is with the Canal Lands.' And then he sang along with the rest of the verse. The preacher answered only with a nod. Tvi!"

"It looked as though the Swedish preacher was embarassed by the Norwegian funeral. He excused himself, saying that he had to travel on. They could take care of the rest of the funeral as well as they could, he said. And with that, he left. Tvi!"

"The Swedish preacher had not gone many paces before the Klokker ran after him with his hymnbook in his fist. He also wanted to give the preacher a reminder about the Canal Lands."

"But Puttekaasen, who was an orderly fellow and wanted everything to go just right, could not put with that kind of interruption to this solemn business. He grabbed the Klokker by the neck and led him back to the grave again and said, 'Tend to business now! Is it the habit of Christian folks to run off in the middle of this business?' Tvi!"

"When the Swedish preacher some time later met some Norwegians, he asked them if it was a common custom among the Norwegians to drink so much at funerals. They answered that Norwegians did usually have a few swigs on such occasions."

" 'Then I will not come to a Norwegian funeral again. No, I will never do it again!' said the Swedish preacher. Tvi!"

Translated by Neil T. Eckstein

JAKE'S WEDDING

Neil T. Eckstein

*IF "JAKE'S WEDDING" has about it an archaic sound—the
sound of a 19th century American story—it is perhaps because it
is a story of what Norwegian immigrants experienced as "the
Yankee thing." Yankees, who tended to appoint themselves as
the prevailing elite and arbiters of good taste in manners and
language had to be reckoned with. In Sinclair Lewis'* Mainstreet
*(1920), New Englander Ezra Stowbody, who came to Gopher
Prairie in 1865, views the fact that Norwegians own stores as an
affront to the Yankees who first arrived in the community. Many
Norwegians refused to take Yankees all that seriously and there is
an old song which notes that it is necessary to say "yes"—not
"yah"—to a Yankee even though you don't agree with him or
think he is just pain "uppity." "Jake's Wedding" presents a more
serious appreciation of the intermarriage of Yankee and
Norwegian—at least by Old Terje, a first-generation immigrant.*

The dulcimer clanging of the old Connecticut clock on the mantel
aroused a flushed response on Lena Norton's excited face. For long weeks she
had waited for this grand moment. In spite of the haste of their courtship, her
Jake now had the audacity to be late! To Lena's prim sense of decorum and
order, the easy-going ways of Jake Larson, immigrant and interloper, were a
source of puzzling exasperation. Late for his own wedding! How very like
Jake that was, and yet she could not bring herself to think of him harshly,
telling herself that she loved him all the more for his casual tardiness.

Just then, her father, Lambert Norton, burst in upon her room with the
news that the Larson party had just arrived. They had slipped in almost
stealthily through the back door—Jake and his parents, Terje and Anne
Larson, his brother Kittel, and his sister, Ragnhild Sveom. Neither Kittel's
wife, Kari, nor Ragnhild Sveom's husband, Anders, came with the groom's
party, in spite of the fact that they had been invited in a most explicit manner.
Somewhere deep in the morasses of the Nordic soul there is a fierce pride
which outlanders can never fathom, and the absence of the two in-laws of Jake
Larson had something to do with that inverted pride which paraded itself as

an excess of humility.

For old Terje Larson and his shawl-draped wife, Anne, the threshold of the Norton house was as formidable as the entrance to the great and gilded throne room of an exalted monarch. Ever since they moved into their little log house, built by their clever sons Jake and Kittel, they had looked up through their narrow-paned windows to the great Yankee house on the hill. The house, gleaming white with apple-green shutters, stood there like a sentry over the entire valley, and in the humble reckoning of poor Terje and Anne, entrance to such a grand place seemed more remote by far then to the promised mansions of Paradise. Yet today they entered that big white house, clothed in their drab and rough homespun, to find themselves suddenly accosted by a gregarious Lambert Norton who extended his fine hand in surprisingly egalitarian fashion into the gnarled paw of startled old Terje.

Will the wonders of this strange America never cease? Only once before in his life, when he had stood rigidly at attention at the garrison in Kristiansand during his young days in the Norwegian militia in the presence of a visiting Swedish general, did Terje feel so overwhelmed by pomp and high status. But today the great Yankee had stretched forth his hand to greet poor Terje as a friend and equal, and had welcomed the groom's party with effusive warmth. His words sounded like so much cackling to the ears of Terje and Anne, but Jake stood by to translate Norton's eloquent words into peasant Norse for his parents. Old Terje, sensing the dignity of the occasion, paused for a moment in the far end of the kitchen, and then intoned a humble greeting in Norse to his host. The guttural peasant voice assaulted the gleaming crystal and the hanging drapes and the genteel horsehair and velvet opulence of the newly refurbished Norton house. The strange, high-pitched utterances of Terje were overheard by the awaiting guests of the Norton family in the great sitting room, and one silk-bedecked Norton dowager, the widow of Lambert Norton's deceased older brother, Harry, was heard to mutter disdainfully to her daughter, "I suppose that man was speaking Norwegian. What a strange and disgusting language it really is. Lena might have found herself a nice Yankee beau instead of this foreigner she insists upon marrying!"

But Harry Norton's widow spoke her words so cautiously that even her daughter had difficulty hearing them, and her daughter softly reproved her mother, pointing out that the tall, handsome Jake was easily the match for many a Yankee. Didn't Uncle Lambert himself speak of him with enthusiasm and high regard?

Roberta Bacon did not attend her sister's wedding because she had recently suffered a miscarriage and it would not be wise to make the journey from Fond du Lac in her weakened condition. Jake was relieved when he heard that she would not be there, for he feared meeting her. Somehow it was much better that she was not there. Perhaps Jake was just being protectively cautious about his new love for Lena and did not want it shaken by too sudden a challenge from the old love. This new love was inexplicable, yet beautifully gentle and serene. Lena, simple and good-hearted as she was, had soon overcome Jake's reserve and caution and they had opened to each other as old friends and companions, and the friendship had quickly ripened into a full-blown love. No one was more surprised than Lambert Norton when Jake and Lena accosted him one evening and told him of their discovered love and their resolve to become man and wife. The startled Norton could offer no objection, but stuttered some approving remarks to mask his complete surprise. In a way, it was all a kind of sweet nemesis for Jake to see Norton so completely taken aback.

But today, on Lena's wedding day, Lambert Norton was in fine form, ushering the Larson parents into velvet plush seats in the parlor. With the parents sat their daughter, Ragnhild Sveom, tan-faced and thin. Norton smiled as he saw Ragnhild's fingers caress the soft velvet of the chair upon which she was sitting. In poor Ragnhild's life there had been very little soft velvet to caress. Even now, in this relaxed moment, her face seemed drawn and her body hard and calloused by endless and demanding work.

By the broad-arched doorway stood Jake with his brother Kittel. Kittel, older than Jake by two years, was red-faced and bearded, in striking contrast to the beardless and blond Jake.

At the mantel the Rev. Ezekiel Jackson stood, a Methodist preacher who occasionally conducted preaching services in Knott's schoolhouse, just one short mile away from the Norton house on the east road. Tall and awkward in appearance. Ezekiel Jackson's greatest endowment was a pious nasal drone which greatly impressed some of his more susceptible listeners. Mr. Jackson had ridden almost forty miles on his black and somewhat aging mare in order to perform this marriage of Lena Norton and the young Scandinavian stranger. But old Terje Larson looked at Mr. Jackson with eyes of suspicion. How could a marriage be truly valid if the minister wore neither ruff nor gown? He had been assured beforehand that the Rev. Mr. Jackson was as genuinely a Yankee preacher as Nils Brandt was truly a Norwegian "prest," yet Terje still had lingering doubts about Jackson's legitimacy and authority to perform this marriage.

The Rev. Mr. Jackson's stance at the mantel was the pre-arranged signal for the commencement of the wedding. Lambert Norton vanished temporarily up the stairway and in a few moments emerged with his daughter Lena upon his arm. She was dressed very simply in a brown silk dress, and her light brown hair was parted severely in the middle and pulled back tightly. Flushed and nervous, she nearly tripped on the stairs, and then she caught the eye of her bridegroom who was waiting for her at the landing. Shyly she smiled, then reddened with a blush as she took Jake's arm. Together they walked into the parlor and stood before the parson. Kittel Larson stood by the side of his brother, and Lena's cousin, Sophie Norton, daughter of the deceased Harry Norton, rose from her chair in the corner to stand by Lena's side.

Mr. Jackson read from a worn and tattered black book, entoning the vows with a kind of ominous chant. Old Terje wondered if this Yankee preacher was really trying to chant and couldn't bring it off, or if this was just the Yankee way of preaching. Next to the ruff and the gown, chanting was the mark of a true "prest" in the mind of Terje, and this poor stick of a Yankee preacher put on a poor performance, to be sure. Why, back in Austre Møland Church, in the days of old Pastor Sandberg, there was some real chanting then. Folks said that Sandberg chanted to put the devil asleep, and Terje was inclined to believe it. But in America it was different. Even the Norwegian preachers here weren't so great on chanting. Brandt really wasn't much good at it, although he tried, which was more than some of them did ...

In the midst of old Terje's reverie it was suddenly all over, and before he knew what was happening, Lambert Norton handed a fine crystal glass to Terje, filled nearly to the rim with a reddish-brown wine.

"I propose a toast," said Norton to the entire company in a raised voice, "to the bride and the groom. May their days together be long and happy," and winking at old Terje, who understood not a word, he continued, "and may we both live to become grandfathers!"

Terje drank his wine down lustily, somewhat to the embarrassment and amusement of the other guests.

"Fine old Madeira," Norton spoke to Terje, forgetting momentarily that his words would not be understood, "I ordered it from Milwaukee last spring, hoping that I would have a special use for it soon."

At about this time Terje and his wife were escorted to the dining room where they sat down to a long table spread with fine Yankee food.

Old Terje lived nearly ten years after his son's wedding on that October afternoon in 1866. Often, in the months and years which followed, old Terje would look through the narrow panes of his log house and see the large white Norton house on the hill with its apple-green shutters, just about a half a mile north of his own small home, and he would reminisce about the wedding of his son. He would think about all that velvet and fine crystal that was up there, and then he would smile contentedly that he had once been an honored guest at that great house. But in all the ten years after the wedding he never received another invitation to that house, nor did he ever expect to receive one. In his later years he was concentrating his thinking upon more distant mansions. One April day, in 1876, when he was thinking along these lines, he suddenly felt a great pain, and then, almost as suddenly, he died with a smile on his lips. It seemed to old Terje that the very last thing that he could taste was Madeira wine out of a beautiful crystal goblet.

THREE STORIES

Norman Reitan

ACCORDING TO Rolf Erickson, who made these stories available for this anthology, Reitan wrote Bright Patches, *the autobiography from which the following stories are taken, between 1936 and 1940. The autobiography has not yet been published.*

Reitan was the son of a Norwegian immigrant who settled in a Norwegian community in Shawano County, Wisconsin. Because many of his family memories were painful ones, Reitan invented or modified names of characters and created stories or "episodes" which seem to be fictional. Reitan's own rebellion against paternal authority is revealed not only in the subjects and themes of these stories but also in the droll and ironic manner in which they are told.

1. OLAF

My father, Peter Johanson Øien, was the oldest son in the Øien family and under the rule of primogeniture which prevailed in Norway was in line to inherit the Øien gaard. In the late sixties, however, there occurred one of those waves of emigration to America and my father, then a lad of nineteen, resolved to go also. It was considered the thing to do at that time, especially for a young man of parts, full of enterprise and energy. Besides, his own father was in good health and it seemed likely would remain in active possession of the gaard for many years to come. He could remain in America a few years, save his money, and when the time came, return to this patrimony with enough capital so that he could improve and modernize the farm and put it on a paying basis. Actual cash had not been too plentiful in the Øien family of late years and a bit of American gold could work wonders. Such were his plans, then, when my father set out for the land of opportunity.

Here, after some years, he came to the town of Lessor, near Shawano, Wisconsin, where he met and married my mother and bought the land, on the shores of White Lake, which was to become the farm home.

He set to work at once to carve a farm out of the wilderness, to hew down a hardwood forest single-handed, to build a habitation for his little family and a shelter for his few animals. But he had scarcely begun when a letter came from his mother in Norway telling him of the sudden death of his father and urging him to return and claim what was his own. This was what he had known must come some day, but now that it had happened he realized that he had begun to take root in this new country and that it was not quite as simple and easy to go away as he had thought when he planned it all from the beginning. Yet his duty seemed plain, and where duty was involved my father was never a man to hesitate. With his wife and two children he sailed back to Norway.

He remained there four years. He did his best to become a part of the life of those among whom he had been raised and to forget the interlude he had spent across the stormy Atlantic, but it was not easy. Things which had once seemed right and proper now wore an utterly different aspect. He became restless and his thoughts often were far away. And for my mother it was far worse . Though born in America, she was of Norwegian parentage and learned the language before she learned English. My father had hoped she would find Norway a real home, but she had grown up as a pioneer, had become inured to the hardships of pioneer life and now pined for what she had left behind. She found the life in her fatherland slow, smug and complacent. And Grandma Øien did not help matters much, for, though she intended to be kind to her, she secretly resented the fact that her favorite son had brought home an "American" wife and she was unable wholly to conceal this. Mother felt this keenly and chafed at having to assume a role of complete subserviency in the household. Grandma Øien brooked no questioning of her authority.

Time passed and things grew no better. Neither of my parents was happy, and at last my father came to see that no really satisfactory adjustment was ever likely to come about. My mother, usually so meek and uncomplaining, grew more and more rebellious and insistent upon a return to America. In the end, Father overcame his scruples about duty and yielded. It was with inner satisfaction and relief that he finally decided to forsake the land of his birth and returned permanently to America and Wisconsin.

By this time the family had increased to four children, two boys and two girls. The third child, a boy named Olaf, had completely won the heart of his grandmother and she found the thought of giving him up quite intolerable. She was deeply grieved that my father could find it in his heart to leave family and heritage and go away once more to the ends of the earth. That was hard enough, surely, she said, for her to have to bear in her declining years, but no one should take her beloved grandchild from her. She clung to the child with a fierce and passionate tenderness. My parents felt the justice of her claim and though the parting cost real pain to both of them, and especially Mother, the boy was left behind in Norway, with the understanding that he was to come to America and rejoin his family when he had grown to manhood.

25

Grandma Øien and her two daughters (with whom Olaf lived after her death) idolized the lad. He was never subjected to the stern repression that is the lot of most European children. He grew up to think of his grandmother and his aunts as comrades, as his equals, the same as his boyhood chums. He was encouraged to express himself freely and fearlessly and was never rebuked or rebuffed for a want of reverence towards his elders.

During these years my father sent considerable financial aid from America, and at times it was sorely needed. Olaf's two aunts, as the years passed, idealized their absent brother more and more. He came to take on the attributes of a mythical, half-remembered hero, and they filled the mind of the growing boy with tales of his father's great virtues and nobility. Olaf read the story of John Halifax and identified his father with its central character.

Olaf, like his father before him, was nineteen when he watched the rugged coast of Norway disappear beneath the eastern horizon. His young heart swelled as the long journey drew towards its end and the hour of reunion came nearer. He yearned toward these parents from whom he had been separated so many years and toward the seven brothers and sisters whom he had never seen. His imagination painted a glowing picture of the idyllic family life into which he was so soon to enter and to be welcomed.

That welcome, when it came at last, was as warm and heart-felt as young Olaf had anticipated, but almost at once he began to sense that things here were not as he had pictured them. My father's household was governed very differently from that in which the boy had grown up in Norway. This American branch of the Øien family was conducted along strictly patriarchal lines. My father's word was law and no one seemed ever to have dreamed of questioning it. His rule was kindly, for the most part, but completely autocratic. He dispensed unswerving justice—at least according to his own lights—but he took no counsel of those he ruled and at times displayed an imperious temper.

Young Olaf found this stern parent very different from the shining hero he had been brought up to revere. He felt it to be a bit incongruous that, in a land where democracy was almost a religion, his role should be one of complete submission to the will of another. He was a high-spirited youngster, and he very soon found such a role quite beyond him.

The elder Øien held the family to be the most sacred of all human institutions and he was utterly convinced that implicit obedience to the family head was the foundation rock of that institution. This conviction had become even more firmly fixed as the years passed. As yet no other son had grown to manhood and my father had known no oppositon to his will within his family. The three children brought back from Norway had all perished of black diptheria, one on the voyage, the other two soon after its completion. When Olaf came to America, Johan was the eldest surviving son and he was but a lad of nine. There were daughters almost grown to young womanhood by now, but it had probably never occurred to them to question their father's authority.

With young Olaf, though, it was quite different. By temperament he tended to question any authority and he had a very well-developed will of his own.

Almost from the first hour there was tension between father and son—little sources of irritation kept springing up. Olaf threw himself into the farm work at once and worked with a will, but he had learned to do things one way and his father had become used to doing them in another. The older man was quick to criticize, the younger quick to resent what seemed to him the arbitrary and intolerant way in which the criticism was offered. The second day they were in the field together Father called Olaf's attention to the fact that the strap was not drawn tight enough on the hames, pointing out that this could lead to chafing and gall sores. Instead of accepting this rebuke in silence, Olaf retorted promptly that Father's own harness had been in the same condition the previous day. Father stopped in his tracks and looked hard at this audacious stripling; for a moment it seemed there might be a crisis at once, but the boy did not quail before his gaze and the older man kept his temper in check. In fact, to do him justice, Father must have exercised an enormous amount of self-control during those next few months. No doubt about it, he truly loved this big, handsome son whom he scarcely knew, and he wanted no clash. He could not always restrain his tongue, but he kept an iron grip on his passion—he who never before had been "answered back" by a child of his own flesh.

The boy, too, tried hard to curb his resentment and to keep the peace between the two of them. His mother, who understood both their natures, pleaded with him to yield to his father in all things, to humor him and never to cross him. Yet even on those occasions when his father vouchsafed no actual criticism, the young man often felt the strong disapproval of the parent and it irked him almost beyond endurance.

In the autumn, Father consented to send Olaf to Scandinavia Academy, which was a strong Lutheran school at no great distance and where Father felt sure his son's spiritual welfare would not suffer. Olaf was anxious to get on with his English and made a splendid record at the school. He was an outstanding success socially, as well, for he was handsome and jovial and with a cheery word for everyone. When he came home for the Christmas holidays, he proudly displayed a trumpet which he had acquired and learned in order to play in the school band. But his exuberance was soon dampened at this point, for his father took sharp exception to the expenditure of hard-earned money on such a piece of frivolity as this trumpet.

After that Olaf accepted no more money from his father for school expenses; he insisted on working his way entirely. The following summer, instead of coming back to the farm, he set out as a house-to-house canvasser, selling stereopticon sets, and did amazingly well at it. He began his second year at Scandinavia with a tidy sum to his credit and with a wardrobe quite as up-to-date and as well-chosen as that of any of his classmates. He remained on cordial terms with his family during this latter time, visiting at the farm as frequently as he could for week-ends and at odd times, but he was paddling his own canoe now and he obviously proposed to steer it too.

Father made no effort to exact a complete obedience from him now. He was hurt by this assertion of independence, a little at a loss to understand just how it had all come about, but accepted the situation gravely and without spoken protest. Mother was unhappy about it all, but felt herself helpless.

But it was essentially a truce rather than a peace. Given the temperament of these two men, some sort of a break was bound to come sooner or later. It came during the second Christmas season.

The younger children regarded Olaf with a half-shy admiration, almost with awe, when they thought of his daring. Johan in particular strove to emulate him in every possible way. He tried his best to copy Olaf's little mannerisms and to walk with Olaf's jaunty swagger. For the first time in his life, also, Johan began to be conscious of his appearance and his apparel. He studied earnestly the way his older brother made use of a comb and brushes and then set to work manfully to reduce his own unruly locks to some sort of submission so he could part his hair exactly the way Olaf parted his.

It was noon of a snapping cold December day. Father had been cutting wood all forenoon and was hungry. Dinner had been called and he stood at table, impatiently waiting for the rest of the family to assemble. No meal could begin without prayer, and prayer could not be offered until everyone was present. At last all were in their places, save only little Johan, who lingered in the washroom while he doused his obstinate cowlick with water and struggled to make his hair look like Olaf's.

Father called to him in irritation to stop primping and get to the table. Olaf came promptly to the defense of his young worshipper.

"You might at least let the boy be clean and neat if he wants to be," he said.

A little gasp from Mother and the girls. Olaf had never before presumed to go so far as this. The brow of the head of the house of Øien grew black as he glared at his eldest son, and he gripped the back of his chair until his knuckles showed white. Then, with a mighty effort of will, he regained mastery of himself and after a moment of silence began the prayer. His voice trembled a little as he asked his heavenly Father to bless their simple meal and to let His wisdom shine in upon the hearts of those of His children who were sorely troubled. The hymn was omitted; he seemed not to trust himself quite that far.

No one ventured to speak as we began the meal. Father's hunger seemed to have left him, for he ate very little. Twice he left the table without a word, going into an adjoining room and closing the door behind him. When one of the younger children timidly asked Mother why Father was acting like this, Mother replied in a frightened whisper, "He's gone in there to pray."

When the meal was finally at an end and everyone rose, Father laid his hand on Olaf's shoulder and said quietly, "Come in here, I want to talk to you." Olaf followed him without a word and the two disappeared.

Exactly what was said during that fateful interview we have never known. Father never referred to it in later years. Olaf was also reluctant to discuss it, though he did tell his mother, and later Johan, a little. About all we know for certain is that Father told the young Scandinavia senior that they had reached a parting of the ways. No son of his should ever again interfere between him and his family. Olaf must acknowledge that he had been wrong and in the future change his whole attitude or he must cease to regard himself as a member of the Øien family.

Father undoubtedly went much farther than he had intended, said things which he never ceased to regret. His wrath had been pent up for a long time. Certain it is that an ultimatum was not the approach to use when dealing with a son like this one.

Olaf did not answer his father in kind, but he left the farm home at once. A few months later he migrated to California and was seen no more by most of his family. Mother grieved for him as long as she lived. I do not believe Father had ever seriously considered the possibility that his son would not yield, and when he did *not* yield it was a staggering blow. In the years that followed I have no doubt that he often longed for his absent son and wished devoutly he could crush his pride and reclaim him, but his pride was too great and there was never a reconciliation between them.

In the spring of 1910 a wire came, telling us that Olaf was near death and that he was asking for his sister Christina, of whom he had always been particularly fond. She left immediately, but before she had time to reach him a second wire came, announcing Olaf's death.

Father seemed utterly crushed by this blow. He had borne the loss of other sons and daughters with a certain amount of stoicism and Christian resignation. Though he had grieved deeply on each of these former occasions, he had always managed to bear his sorrow with silent fortitude, not permitting even the members of his immediate family to know quite how hard he was hit. He was able to maintain this outward composure even when his little Thelma was taken from him. She had died at the age of nine, following a ruptured appendix. With competent medical attention she might very well have survived that illness and grown into the glorious womanhood that she already gave promise of, but the only available doctor bungled everything, wrung his hands helplessly, and let her die. The sweetness of this child had endeared her to everyone; she was the darling and pet of the whole family. This was especially true in the case of her father; there was never any sternness in either tone or look when this little girl was present. When she left us, Father hid his face from his family, but no one saw him weep.

Now, however, he made little or no effort to keep up a front. For a time it seemed his world had crumbled about him. Even the consolation of religion appeared to fail him. It is an appalling thing to see a man break down and go to pieces as Father did during those first few weeks. It was many days before he could speak without his voice breaking and it was years before he could refer to his estranged son without betraying evidence of the bitter grief that still gnawed within him.

In 1915 he made a journey to the Pacific Coast, ostensibly to visit a cousin living out there. The house which this cousin occupied was near a spot where Olaf lay buried. Day after day Father found some excuse or other to postpone a visit to the grave. He was nerving himself for what he knew must prove a harrowing ordeal. Then at last he announced one morning that he was ready to visit the cemetery where his son slept. He seemed almost cheerful and conversed quite calmly during the short drive. He alighted from the little automobile and walked to the grave with every appearance of firmness and resolution. But when he could make out the letters on the little tombstone, his body began to tremble and his face to work uncontrollably. After a moment, he threw himself face down upon the grave and fairly groveled in the awful agony of his spirit. The cousin told Johan about it a year or two later, adding that it had been one of the most shattering experiences he himself had ever gone through.

So this tragedy of misunderstanding and pride and frustrated love played itself out to its end. It took a heavy toll from all who had a part in it, yet in the end I believe it had a mellowing effect upon Father and upon the whole family. Father was never again quite the autocrat he had been before the break with Olaf. I have noticed many times during these last years that, when one of the older brothers or sisters recounts anecdotes of our early family life, the impression one gets of my father is one of sternness and austerity. But there is very little of this in the memories which the youngest three of four still preserve of their father. In the last years much of the narrowness and intolerance left him. I am glad that most of my own boyhood came during this last phase.

2. POINT OF HONOR

Sven Nygard was a hell-raiser all his life. He started as an obstreperous infant, became an incorrigible child, a profligate youth, and finally a dissolute man. There were no interludes of reform. Sven was consistent, if nothing else.

When scarcely more than a baby, he discovered that pulling the wings from flies was a highly amusing sport. A few years later he learned to trap birds, pull out their tail feathers and then set them free again, observing, with great interest, their futile attempts to steer their flight. He became the ringleader of a set of reckless young scalawags who made it their business to see to it that life did not become too placid and monotonous for the rest of the countryside. No watermelon patch or chicken coop was ever safe from the maraudings, and they seemed never at a loss when it came to stirring up some new form of deviltry. Once they threw a peaceful, Saturday-night barn dance into pandemonium by waving a flaming branch before the window and shrieking "Fire!" at the tops of their lusty voices. On another occasion four of these young wastrels, Sven at their head, rode their ponies into Cedarville, opened the gates of the well-filled stock pens, and drove a terrified mass of calves, hogs, and cattle pell-mell through the crowded main street. The bewildered animals snorted and squealed and bleated, the hoofs of the pursuing ponies clattered, their riders keeping up a continual whooping, and the populace was scattered in all directions in wild panic.

He grew up to be a handsome lad, with a way about him that few could resist. Mothers warned their daughters and issued stern edicts; this young Lothario was to be given a wide berth. But, as often happens under such circumstances, this made him all the more attractive and desirable, so that, in a number of instances, the warnings were wasted and the edicts disregarded. For Sven had a bold, roving eye, a boundless impudence and a gay, swaggering manner that proved all but irresistible to feminine hearts. He cut a wide swath among the young ladies of the neighborhood and left a trail of broken hearts behind him. Once he tasted triumph, he lost all interest and passed immediately on to the next conquest.

While still very young, he acquired a liking for liquor, and the habit fastened itself more and more strongly upon him as he grew older. Toward the last, he gave up almost everything in order to concentrate on his drinking, even neglecting his other vices.

He was a big, powerful man and when he reached a certain stage in the progress of his carousing he invariably felt the need for physical combat. More than once he was known to have "cleaned out" a whole saloon. Many of his major sprees ended in the county jail because of this proclivity for brawling.

Ours was a church-going community, so much so that the absence of anyone from a regular service was promptly noted by his neighbors. Only illness or something equally serious could possibly justify such an absence. But the pressure of public disapproal had little or no effect upon Sven; he would have none of this sitting in a stuffy church and drowsing through a long-winded exhortation when there were so many other intersting things to do. Hunting, courting, gambling or drinking—all offered far more lively entertainment for Sven.

Once the minister cornered him and lectured him at some length upon the awful peril in which his soul rested. Sven listened good-humoredly but was quite unimpressed. At the end of the diatribe, he stood up, reached down and pulled the little clergyman to his feet, clapped him on the back and invited him cordially to come with him and have a drink. The next Sunday Sven was used as the subject of the sermon. He, declared the preacher, offered a horrible example of a soul headed straight for inevitable damnation. When Sven heard about it, he laughed uproariously and retold it to his saloon cronies as a fine joke.

Yet, with all his shortcomings, Sven had one redeeming virtue. In money matters he was scrupulously honest. Never did a debt, either for money or for a favor, go unpaid. When he was on a spree and his money ran out he would buy more liquor on credit (which was always extended to him freely), but after that particular carouse was over he would work hard and save his money and pay every penny of what he owed before going off on another orgy. And never did a man do Sven a favor, but Sven found some way to return it—with interest.

One day, when he was in his late fifties, Sven drank too much raw alcohol. He collapsed and they carried him to an upstairs room and laid him on a couch. It was thought he would sleep it off, but as time passed, the saloon-keeper, who had known Sven all his life and had a great fondness for him, in spite of the chairs and tables he had wrecked, became a little uneasy. Toward night, he slipped away from the bar, lighted a kerosene lamp and tiptoed up to have a look at his old friend. As the yellowish light fell upon the face of the prostrate man, the saloon-keeper knew instantly, and with a great shock, that Sven Nygard was very near the end of his earthly sojourn. He rushed downstairs and dispatched his two sons in all haste, one for the doctor and the other for the minister. The doctor was miles away on an obstetrics case and was not expected back for many hours. But the Reverend Mr. Guttman, his heart beating high with hope of rescuing a soul from the very jaws of a waiting hell, came as fast as his doughty little mare could cover the distance.

The saloon-keeper brought him into the room where the great form lay crumpled on the couch and withdrew so that they might be alone together.

Gently the minister spoke to Sven, telling him that he could do nothing for his earthly body but that it was not too late, even now, to save his undying soul. He read, by the flickering light of the old lamp, that passage from the New Testament in which is recounted so movingly the words of the Savior to the dying robber on the Cross. If Sven would but repent, but breathe a word of prayer, he might even now avert the terrible doom that otherwise awaited him. In a few short hours, perhaps, he might find himself either in Paradise or in the depths of the fiery pit. Earnestly he entreated the dying man to soften his heart and give himself to Jesus.

Sven listened without comment. When the minister stopped speaking, he remained silent for some time, apparently in deep thought. Then he asked the good man to leave him alone for half an hour that he might consider what he ought to do.

During the next thirty minutes, except for occasional spasms of pain, Sven lay quietly, staring into space. When the minister returned, he was very near death. He made a weak sign for his visitor to bend very close so that the effort of speaking might not be more than his strength could bear. Then, in a voice which was steady and resolute, though barely audible, he said:

"Mr. Guttman, you are a guid man. I know you try to do me big favor now. But I guess it yust can't be dat vay. All my life I pay for da t'ings I get and da t'ings I do. I break all God's laws and have laut of fun doing it. Now it comes time I should pay. I be God damned if I try to get out of it."

3. SCHISM

As a strict Lutheran, my father could not question the doctrine of that church to the effect that if, in the last moments of his life, a sinner but repented and asked God for forgiveness, his soul was admitted to the eternal Paradise, instead of being hurled into the depths of everlasting Hellfire, which would otherwise have been his lot. He had very little faith, however, in the sincerity of most last-minute repentances. If a repentance were not sincere, it was, of course, to no avail. He felt that in many cases—probably in most of them—the alleged repentance had a decidedly ulterior motive; that is, it was an eleventh-hour bargain to gain salvation and not a manifestation of genuine regret for the evil life which the departing one had led.

Though there was no question in my father's mind that Sven Nygard was among the eternally damned, I am convinced that, in his secret heart, he rather admired that notorious roisterer for his refusal to buy his salvation at the last moment at the cost of his self-respect.

My father's religious philosophy was that the only certain road to eternal blessedness was the hard one; one must, during every hour of life, pursue a course of uncompromising rectitude and unwavering piety. Even then one must constantly ask God for forgiveness for the minor transgressions, the wayward thoughts, and the omissions that fill even the most sanctified life. He strove mightily to live according to this philosophy.

The Rev. Albert Anderson, pastor of the church to which my father belonged, considered himself to be as good a Christian and as staunch a Lutheran as any in his flock, but he had no such doubts as to the efficacy of the death-bed repentance. He took no little pride in the number of souls he had literally snatched from the jaws of Hell.

Father believed that alcohol was one of the greatest curses ever to fall upon mankind. To him the use of strong drink in any form was a sin and drunkenness was a mortal sin. The Rev. Mr. Anderson held that temperance consisted in the temperate use of spirits, not in complete abstinence from them. Drunkenness was certainly not to be encouraged, but Mr. Anderson felt that it was a fault God would have little difficulty in forgiving if there was the proper repentance, even at the last gasp of life.

Father did all he could to promote what he believed to be the only real temperance by talking against the Demon Rum on all possible occasions and by arranging for temperance meetings and even financing lectures on the subject.

Another thing that was dear to my father's heart was the week-day prayer meeting. Rev. Anderson felt that if he prepared a reasonably good sermon during the week, delivered it on Sunday, and made a fair number of calls upon those who needed comfort or advice he had done all that was necessary. He was friendly enough, even jovial at times, and liked to meet people, but too much communion with them on a strictly spiritual plane rather bored him. He cared very little for the emotionalism that so often made its appearance at these meetings where people got up and "testified" and made long-winded prayers, often, as it seemed, mainly in order to display their own piety to neighbors who were in no position to escape. When my father insisted on calling these meetings, even though the minister could not be present, Rev. Anderson felt real resentment and began to suspect that perhaps the little church at Oakdale was not big enough to hold both himself and this troublesome parishioner. Both men were entirely sincere, but there seemed no common ground on which they could meet and agree.

When Magnus Svenson died in a drunken paroxysm, my father expected a funeral sermon of dire warning, holding up Magnus as a terrible example of a soul which had been taken in deadly sin and had been consigned straight to perdition. Rev. Anderson was more concerned about the feelings of the bereaved family than about frightening the rest of the congregation. He had no wish to embarrass anyone and besides he believed in giving every soul the benefit of any possible doubt. So, turning a deaf ear to Father's suggestions, he said, in the course of the funeral service, "We must hope that, before he died, he breathed a prayer, asking for forgiveness, and that his soul had therefore gone safely home to his Maker."

Father was deeply incensed; his whole being revolted at this craven evasion of the issue. For a minister of God to mince words at such a time, to shrink from his plain duty, was not only craven, but a breach of faith toward both his parishioners and his God. Furthermore, it was little short of rank heresy. No one denied that Magnus had died in a drunken fit. For this minister to try to slip him into heaven by what was little better than a sleight-of-hand trick was to give open countenance to all manner of debauchery. He might as well come right out and say to his flock: "Live a life of sin and wickedness if you must, but at all events be of good cheer. I will get you into Heaven some way, never fear." This funeral sermon was the last to which Father listened in the Oakdale church for many years. He realized that a majority of the church membership were on the minister's side—or at least were not willing to take any definite stand against him. So with a heavy heart, and after much prayer and inner conflict, Father resigned. It cost him heavily to take this step, for the church meant a good deal to him.

His father-in-law shook his white head and said sadly: "Peter, Peter—you shouldn't have done it. You will regret it as long as you live." To which Father replied grimly that he was not planning to get along without a church, but would build a new one. With the Øiens went half a score of other families out of the Oakdale church. These were mostly from the western side of the parish, friends and neighbors of many years standing. Within a year or two, this compact nucleus drew to itself quite a few recruits, some of them journeying a consider-

34

able distance to be present at the meetings. Father went so far as to secure a lot as a site for the new church and even began cutting logs, but then it was decided that until the little congregation grew the schoolhouse at Stadland would do very well as a place of worship.

The services of a minister were secured for every fourth Sunday. He owed allegiance to a different synod than Mr. Anderson—one whose tenets were somewhat more in accord with the views of this hardy little band. On the other three Sundays, each family held services in its own home, or gathered informally to pray and worship together, or perhaps listened to some itinerant evangelist. Several week-night prayer meetings were often held during the course of the month and though the attendance at some of these might be very sparse, especially when the weather was inclement, those who came made up in fervor what they lacked in number. It was as my father said, "Where two or three are gathered together in My name, there am I in the midst of them." But the red letter days were the Sundays when the little congregation had its own minister on hand to preach to it. He had four churches, widely scattered, and travelled from one to the next by train. Clergymen were given half-fare rates in those days and they needed every concession they could obtain, for their pay was meagre. Our minister would arrive on Saturday, or even Friday, and would be met at Cecil and driven to our home, where he would be received and treated as the guest of honor. Father enjoyed enormously the long discussions of theology and doctrine which he could have with these men during the evenings which they spent under our roof. Services at the little schoolhouse began at ten on Sunday morning and Father would have been deeply mortified had we not all been in our places before that hour. Getting us all there on time often involved some rather frantic bustling about. Ordinarily, we breakfasted soon after seven, but of course no one might sit down to the breakfast table before the preacher had put in his appearance and the worthy man sometimes failed to appear until long past eight. Our parents would not dream of having such a guest awakened; that would have shown a lack of respect and consideration. Poor Johan, who had risen at five and rushed through the milking and the other necessary chores of Sunday morning, found this delay of breakfast especially trying.

The Sunday morning services lasted a full two hours or more, but when the long sermon at last came to an end and the words of benediction had been pronounced, there were always a few minutes of visiting and handshaking, which almost everyone looked forward to eagerly. Some of these people saw each other only on these fourth-Sunday occasions and there was much that needed telling and exclaiming over. If it was too bitter cold, the children took advantage of this time to run about a little and stretch their cramped legs.

Many times Father would announce that all who cared to would be welcome at the Øien home for dinner and afternoon worship. A goodly number accepted, especially those who had driven some distance. It was possible to seat thirty guests in our home, by using all the chairs and all the tables, and every seat was usually occupied. Much of the preparation had been made the day before and when the little procession from the schoolhouse drove into the farmyard, every woman seized an apron and made for the kitchen. The men occupied themselves with unhitching and caring for the animals, and by the time this was finished the meal was almost ready. Those bountiful, leisurely Sunday dinners, with the good fellowship which they engendered, were something to be long remembered. These hard-working, God-fearing farmers and their wives were able to relax and to discourse without hurry or fret. They made the most of it. But at last there would come the scraping of chairs, which announced that the grown-ups had finished their meal and were about to surrender the table. It was a most welcome sound to the score or more of youngsters who were waiting their turn. When our elders sat down we knew from experience that there would be a long wait, and for the first hour or so we managed to keep ourselves occupied, romping about the yard and playing games; but toward the latter end of the feast inside our stomachs always grew clamorous and we pressed close to the dining room door, awaiting the signal to rush in pell-mell.

"Here, Johnny," some woman would call out, "here's where your mother sat. You can sit right here and go ahead." Clearing the table and putting on all clean dishes would have taken an unthinkable amount of time—even if there had been that many clean dishes available. Kindly women hurried back and forth from kitchen to table, bringing on more hot food and seeing to it that hungry mouths were filled. Food vanished as does green vegetation when a swarm of locusts settles down upon a field. We had as merry and satisfactory a time at the table as had our elders. We were never asked to maintain a decorous silence at such times, even though it was Sunday. Our parents were deeply religious, but they were not Puritans, in the unpleasant sense.

So the little rebel congregation carried on, for almost ten years. Many of Peter Øien's children were confirmed in the schoolhouse at Stadland and passed a good share of their childhood knowing no other church. But as the years went by the congregation began to dwindle. Hans Hanson and his family of eleven children moved to Minnesota; Ole Stolen and Eric Johnson and Hjalmar Thorson and John Dahl and John Bakken died. Old Chris Jorgenson became too infirm to come to meetings any longer. One or two other families drifted back to the Oakdale church. It became harder to raise money for church expenses.

And then at last came a change in the Oakdale church itself. The Rev. Mr. Anderson retired, and his successor was more to my father's liking. Perhaps the new pastor was not as uncompromisingly rigid in his doctrine as my father would have demanded ten years earlier, but Father had mellowed and grown more tolerant. A few weeks after the new man took up his duties in Oakdale the reconciliation took place and the remnants of the Stadland band returned to the bosom of the home church at Oakdale. In the privacy of her home, Mother shed tears of happiness.

WHEN BJORNSON CAME TO LA CROSSE

Johannes B. Wist

TRANSLATOR'S NOTE: The general reader may need some information. Bjornstjerne Bjornson (1832-1910), Norway's great poet, was also a novelist, a playwright, and a tireless supporter of causes, one of which was that of the common people, whom he reached through matchless oratory. In middle age he turned from Christianity to a Darwinistic view; this upset and confused his less worldly admirers. His lecture trip to America, where many pious Norwegians had settled, caused immediate strife. While the people loved him and could recite his poems, their consequential ministers all but forbade them to go to his lectures. What often resulted can be found in the present story. Bjornson was here a century ago; thirty years later the memory of that visit had not died and Wist was able to draw upon it. Johannes B. Wist (1864-1923) was one of the best and best known of the Norwegian-American writers. "Da Bjornson kom til La Crosse" appeared in the April 1913 issue of Symra, *a literary magazine published in Decorah, Iowa. I first learned of the story in the writings of Einar Haugen, who called it "a priceless sketch." To read it was to agree, and translation soon followed. Dr. Haugen (emeritus Victor S. Thomas professor of Scandinavian and linguistics in Harvard University) was kind enough to annotate my work; I thank him for his help, the like of which no one else could have offered.*
— Rodney Nelson

In those days, notable visitors from Norway were rarer than they are now. Therefore, when it was learned in the settlement that Bjornson was soon to come to La Crosse to give a lecture, Nils Lorenson Vangseidet was among the first to promise himself and his wife that they would go there even if it cost him the last dollar he had.

Nils had read about it in *Skandinaven*, so he knew that it was true: in his eyes there was nothing so infallible in this world as *Skandinaven*—except, of course, *Truth to Piety*.

It happened that there were not infrequent disagreements between neighbors as to the reliability of this paper. Some of the settlers didn't like *Skandinaven* at all and believed just as firmly in *Homeland and Emigrant* or *Norden* as Nils believed in *Skandinaven*.

Now *Decorah-Posten* had also begun to circulate widely among them, and there were many who favored this publication because it didn't meddle in politics or church controversy. Thus Nils had a sizable party opposing him; sometimes he knew it to his cost. *Skandinaven* was distinguished for one thing only, said his opponents: it contained more squabbling than all of the other newspapers put together.

The two democrats in the settlement read *The Messenger*, and they had to put up with even more than Nils did—*he* had quite a few fellow subscribers. People even said that the two *Messenger* characters still paid allegiance to Negro slavery, in spite of the fact that it had been abolished fourteen or fifteen years ago. This was undoubtedly a terrible exaggeration, yet it was repeated so often that to the popular consciousness it became fact. It was not often that people met each other without giving vent to the wrath that had arisen because of their differences of opinion concerning the press.

But Nils Vangseidet stuck to his belief. Where newspapers were concerned, *Skandinaven* was and would remain his household god. And now too he had read there that B.B. would be coming, and that was a man he wanted to see and hear. Nothing could move him from his resolution.

"Bjornson is the greatest man in Norway, *vet du!*" he said to his wife. "And those that have heard him make a speech say that he's got a real incredible jaw on him. He speaks like no other living man, they say. It's just like it runs out of him, they say. He speaks so that people just sit there in a cold sweat and think they see trolls and other devilment. But then quick as lightning he can turn around the other way and make them giggle and laugh and hold their stomachs so they don't split in two."

"But I did hear or read something to the effect that he was not to be relied upon in matters of faith," objected Olava.

"Oh that there's only womenfolk talking," answered Nils, "because if he were very mistaken in that regard you can be sure John Anderson would have said so in *Skandinaven*."

"Yes, but wasn't it in *Skandinaven* that a minister wrote about it a little while ago?" Olava continued.

"That I never saw," replied Nils. "It must have been in *Norden* you read that; it would have been just like those there writers to hit upon something nasty to say about a great and good man. Anyhow, he's not speaking about religion, so it's all the same."

More was not said about the matter for a time. Olava did not bring it up

38

again; after all, she secretly looked forward to the trip to La Crosse. There were few amusements to be had in the settlement. Year after year people drudged and puttered around, and every day that came was exactly like the one that had gone before.

Nils and Olava had lived here almost fifteen years now. These tracts had been wooded and untidy when they established their claim, but they had toiled and struggled hard so that finally they had gotten the better of poverty, they had. They felt that at last they were sufficiently well off to allow themselves a few pleasures—if the opportunity arose.

So in the previous May they had gone with all of their children to Barnum's circus, and this had been a great experience both for themselves and the youngsters. Most of all for the latter, naturally; in the evenings they would still play circus out in the kitchen, by turns imitating the elephant, the tiger, the rhinoceros and other monsters of land and sea. Then Carl Olavus was the clown, and Mary the trickrider, and Ole Andreas the animal tamer. Jo, that was fun! Little Kathinka and little Theodore, who were too small to "appear," constituted the public and sat with sparkling eyes and throbbing hearts, always awaiting the next thrill which every time seemed novel and fascinating even though they had already seen it a hundred times.

And if the neighbors happened to be there, the children gave "special performances"—but finally these were curtailed since Lars Jordet's little Jens had, one such solemn occasion, been so unlucky as to break a "foreleg" while playing elephant. The elephant was supposed to do tricks just like the elephant in Barnum's circus, so Jens Jordet, rolling on the kitchen table, rolled the wrong way and came down on his arm. There was no more circus for him, poor kid, and the neighbors began to have misgivings about the whole "show." So now the Vangseidet children had to conduct circuses for themselves. But it was fun anyway. If the parents rarely had a chance to see or do anything new, the children's chances were even rarer.

Last autumn Nils and Olava had interrupted their work and gone to town in order to hear a Norwegian who was giving concerts on the Hardanger fiddle. Unfortunately, they hadn't been able to away the last time Ole Bull appeared in La Crosse. This they truely regretted, the more so because there were many in the settlement who had been there and heard him and never missed an opportunity to reminisce about it. It didn't help to oppose them with the claim that one had heard "Lasse Torbenson from Seljord"— or whatever he called himself. Nils had tried to make it seem that he would much rather hear "an authentic Hardanger fiddler" than one of these "erudite artists" who played things people didn't understand one bit, but he had a hidden feeling that such an argument could not go far. Therefore, he chose to let Bull's worshipers brag all they wanted. But he remembered the humiliation; and now that there was a chance to hear Bjornson, who was a much greater man than Ole Bull, he was not about to sit at home this time and give them any further cause for rejoicing.

But Nils was no diplomat. He was so taken with B.B. that whenever he encountered people he had no other topic of conversation, so it wasn't long before the entire settlement knew that he was a great admirer of the famous poet. Ja, in an unguarded moment Nils had even been tempted to say something that was not entirely in accord with the truth; namely, that he had once heard Bjornson talk in Gjovik—he had even shaken his hand. Olava had certainly given him a look as the ill-considered remark escaped his mouth; but done was done, and now he'd have to uphold his role or be subject to laughter.

"I suppose at that time Bjornson wasn't so terribly old," said Johnsgaard the teacher. "And you must have been even younger. Let me see—he was born in '32 and now we write 1880. You've been in this country since 1860 and were only a little boy when you came over—"

"Yes, it was in the spring of 1860," Nils hurried to say, annoyed that his word should not be credited. This Johnsonsgaard, by the way, had replaced Nils as the parish bellringer; he was also a queer fox whom Nils had never been able to stand. And he didn't have much of a singing voice, even if he had gone to college in Norway.

"Well, well, so you two are old friends," the teacher said cunningly. "He'll surely be glad to meet you again. I've been hearing that he's not such a sociable man anymore. But it goes without saying that one must always acknowledge one's friends."

After this, Nils became a little quieter. It bothered him terribly that anyone should think he lied, he who was otherwise such a good and truthful man and stood so high in the congregation. But done was done; no good to start making concessions now. He felt that in a way he had a right to maintain his little white lie—wasn't it only what people had made of it?—because he had always conducted himself as an honest human being and never cheated a living soul; in contrast to the bellringer who all his days had been a deadbeat and a hypocrite.

Meanwhile the time drew near, and besides Nils there were quite a few people who had decided to go and hear Bjornson. It had become an affair of personal and national honor: anybody who wanted to count for something would have to attend. It certainly wouldn't do, afterwards, to have it thrown in one's face, "Yes, it's true that you're the fellow who didn't hear Bjornson that time he was in La Crosse!" No doubt there were some who were beginning to have scruples because of the religious angle, but as long as the minister said nothing there was little cause to worry; and Reverend Nicolaisen was one to keep a close eye on his parishioners where matters of faith were concerned. This had been shown more than once. He belonged to the old pietistic school and tolerated no foolishness in dogma or in life.

But however that may have been, the minister had at last heard that there was something unusual astir that had to do with B.B.'s forthcoming visit to La Crosse.

One week before the great event it was announced that there would be a meeting of the young people's society; it was the custom in those days that the adults would come as well. The minister would deliver a brief "address to our

40

youth." He spoke of unbelief, using the occasion to warn against false prophets; there were so many of them around just now. One should not be deceived by a person's name and celebrity, for it was those who were famous and called great men by the people who presented the worst danger of all.

Bjornson was never named, but everyone understood the intent. It was as though a damp cloud had settled over the gathering. Few did not feel guilty.

Nils Vangseidet and Tobias Nergard left the church together. At first they were both silent, but finally Nils thought he had to say something.

"What did you think then of the minister's speech, Tobias?" he asked. Such a question was not hard to come up with.

"Aa, that was really quite a speech," answered Tobias.

"Of course—it was the true word of God," Nils admitted. "And his speechmaking ability is nothing to laugh at either."

Another deep silence. Nils was again the one to set the conversation moving.

"Ja, now it's only a week until Bjornson speaks in La Crosse," he remarked cautiously.

"Ja, that's true enough," answered Tobias.

"It's too bad that the man should be such a freethinker," Nils went on. He hadn't wanted to say that vulgar word, but there was simply no way around it.

"Ja, that's true," said Tobias.

"But I have a mind to go and hear him anyhow, I think," Nils continued. He gave Tobias a sidelong glance as though to read the effect of his words.

"Ja, well the two of you are like old friends, you two," answered Tobias. He put his hand to his mouth so that Nils wouldn't see that he was smiling.

Nils caught the sarcasm and said no more. But inwardly he was so provoked that he vowed he would go and hear Bjornson even if the whole settlement stayed at home.

In the meantime, Olava and Tobias' wife Inger were walking past the parsonage. The relations of these two were the opposite of the relations between their men. In the latter instance, it was Nils who was blessed with the powers of speech; Olava was one of the most taciturn people in the country. With Tobias and Inger, on the other hand, it was she who did most of the talking while he was usually content to listen.

And glibness was the word of the day. Inger had been *so* edified by the minister's talk. She had never heard him speak so well before. It had been almost enough to make one cry. What he had said about the false prophets was especially "to the point." And it didn't hurt to be put in mind of the danger of those who run around and mislead unwary souls. The neighboring congregation had once been visited by Mormons, people who had many wives and were infested with every vice and horror. But would you believe that even so there were Lutherans who didn't know any better than to go and hear them! And just the other day she had heard about an outspoken freethinker and renouncer of God—an American they called "Vingerisol"—who had "lectured" in La Crosse.

41

And people had climbed over each other to get in, even though they said he'd charge them a dollar each! Ja, this La Crosse was getting to be a disgusting place—a regular Sodom if there ever was. It was only natural that this here Bjornson from Norway should want to go there, being a disgusting person himself. Jo, people said there was no Christianity left in him.

Inger paused a moment to see how Olava was taking it all. But Olava only lowered her eyes and said nothing. And so the one who had words at her command had to proceed.

"Myself now, I feel it would be a sin and a disgrace if anyone from the congregation were to patronize this Bjornson, especially after what Reverend Nicolaisen said."

Olava was silent as before.

After a couple of minutes Inger spoke up again. "They say that Bjornson and Nils were such good friends in childhood and were in the service together up at Jorstadmoen, so it's only reasonable that Nils should want to go to La Crosse and greet him even though, of course, he doesn't care about what he has to say."

But Olava had no enlightment to offer, and now Nils came and was ready to leave, so the chat was interrupted.

On the way home Nils was surly and of few words. He just sat there isolated in his grim resolve. And since Olava naturally didn't say a word, it became rather still.

Finally the situation got to be too painful for Nils, and he burst out:

"Ja, so have they stuffed your head full of all kinds of stories?"

"Who? Is it Inger you mean?"

"Ja, and all the other gossip-bags."

"*Aa nei*," Olava answered evasively, "there was nothing said in particular."

"*Ja, ja*, they can just say whatever they want now," said Nils. "I'm going to La Crosse anyhow, *jeg da*. And if you want to go with, that's alright with me; if not, I can always find the way home alone *og jeg da*."

Olava thought it would be best if she stayed home. But he could go nevertheless since he was a mind to. And so it was.

Big broad-shouldered and powerful, the poet stood before the large gathering. For a second or two his eagle eyes took the measure of the place. When he began the room shook:

> Brede seil over Nordsjo gaar,
> hoit paa skansen i morgnen staar
> Erling Skjalgsson fra Sole—

Nils, who had been lucky enough to get a seat a short ways back in the hall, was almost afraid; soon he experienced more than once that it was true what people said, the man could put you in a cold sweat. He sat the whole time staring at the giant figure; he felt strange. It was not the talk so much as the man himself that got to you. You seemed so tiny in his presence. But Nils had been able to make out one thing: he surely wasn't talking religion. Well, he poked some fun at

42

ministers and public officials back in Norway, and this made people laugh. But otherwise, thought Nils, there was absolutely nothing that seemed out of turn. For the most part it had to do with reaction and progress in Norway, where there was a stirring in the ranks; he also explained why the small and weak in society should be given their rights. In Nils' unschooled opinion, this was desirable. If B.B. was giving hell to those important office holders in Norway, they were getting no better than they deserved.

When the lecture was over and the interminable applause had died down, Nils emboldened himself to go up and shake hands with Bjornson and thank him for the speech. Others were going up, too. He had traveled a long ways; now he thought he'd have a little satisfaction at the expense of his neighbors, none of whom had been man enough to come along. But when he had elbowed his way through the crowd and stood at last before the eminent man, Nils himself was not entirely free of anxiety.

"Please excuse me," he said, extending his hand. "I am only a poor farmer from out in Wolf Valley, but I have traveled thirty-five miles to hear you so I hoped it would be all right to shake your hand and thank you for the talk."

Bjornson eyed him rather sharply, and Nils felt his knees begin to weaken.

But the poet took his hand and gave it a jerk. It was plain that he was tired. After exchanging a few words with his host Mons Anderson and editor Husher of *Homeland and Emigrant*, who were waiting to escort him out of the hall, he turned to Nils with the following remark:

"So, you're a Norwegian farmer, are you! They tell me that the Norwegian farmers in America are a bunch a fine devils! They'll be even finer once they begin to understand that there are better ways to live than with their noses in the dirt. If only their ministers would let them think their own thoughts, you'd really see something! Goodbye, my man!"

With that he slapped Nils on the shoulder and turned to the next in line.

Nils left. He felt a little disappointed, but it was some consolation to know that he had met Bjornson "in the flesh"; and at least the great man had given him a friendly nod. Maybe he had something to be proud of—in spite of the strange words that had been said. What a way to talk! Come to think of it, exactly what business did this bigshot from Norway have to come over here and set himself up as a judge over poor emigrants who lacked both schooling and knowledge because circumstances were such that they had to slave morning and night to get enough to eat? What would *he* do, the oversized tramp, if *he* were placed in such circumstances? *Ja*, what would he do? He'd seen high class people from Norway who had to go and clean spittoons in the bars. One of them was still known as "the baron" *Aajo*, that was some baron! And religion? Ministers? They had been both a comfort and a blessing in many, many ways. Even Nils, who was a bit of an oppositionist, could tell that much. *Aanei*, it was true after all what Reverend had said about the false prophets! . . . But anyway, Nils had heard Bjornson, and for now that was the important thing. Let the worshipers of Ole Bull come on; he'd have an answer for them!

Nils' journey to La Crosse became a great event in the settlement. It seemed that he had not reckoned entirely amiss in thinking that he would triumph over his enemies by daring to take a trip while others, many of whom had also wanted to go, sat at home.

All winter, whenever people met, the one topic of conversation was B.B.; just as now at the final auction of the ladies' aid society.

The members had been busy for a whole year—sewing and drinking coffee and sewing and chatting and discussing such things as are always to be discussed in a ladies' aid out in the country, where affairs, in those days, were even simpler than they are now. Results did not fail to materialize. They had prepared a great many useful things for the auction. And they'd know what to do with the money that came in. The men of the congregation had ordered an altarpiece from Milwaukee, and naturally it was the women's job to make sure it got paid for. And the women took the task seriously, as women always do.

But if there's going to be a ladies' aid auction, the men will have to be there too; after all, it is the men who carry the money. The Norwegian-American farm wife has not been spoiled. But she is a clever wife who knows how to arrange things whenever there is something to be done for the congregation and the common good. And the men keep up appearances throughout the game, buying, at exorbitant prices, their women's rugs and pillows and embroidered aprons. They even outbid each other in the process; for the coffee is good, the lefse and rommegrot and other Norwegian dishes are exquisite, and good humor is the best means to the end.

Now all had received ample refreshments, both bodily and spiritual. Nicolaisen had read a text from the Bible, they had sung a couple of hymns, they had gorged themselves on good food, and so everyone was deeply pleased with both the world and himself. It was a benign atmosphere, and conversations grew lively. In short, there was every reason to assume that it would be a lucrative auction.

Some of the men, among them Nils and the bellringer—that's what they always called teacher Johnsgaard—had gone off into a corner of the schoolhouse and sat discussing, with great zeal, the election of saints which at the time was occupying everyone's thoughts. But soon the talk moved into safer realms. The other day Nils had sold a mare: this was a subject on which all were knowledgeable. The hog market and the price of wheat were other topics in which every farmer must needs take an interest, and here Nils found another opportunity to attack *Homeland and Emigrant* and *The Messenger* for misrepresenting the state of the market, while *Skandinaven* was as usual an organ of utter truthfulness, in economics as in politics. The conversation then drifted naturally over to politics, and from there it was not hard to slip into religion and the church.

The bellringer held fast to the opinion which he had often expressed earlier: that men like Bjornson and his kind were a great menace to Christianity. "They are cunning as serpents and full of the knowledge and

44

intrigues of this world," he said. For an example of how they could turn the heads of otherwise good and honest people, he hinted with some irony, take Nils Vangseidet—even he had been unable to avoid the influence of Bjornson's talk in La Crosse.

Nils hated the bellringer with an inextinguishable hatred, and immediately the blood rose in him.

"This has gotten to be like the original sin itself," he rejoined. "Here I've told you again and again that there was not one living word about religion in his entire speech, and I should know, I who heard it. Others can say exactly what they want. It's nothing to repent of, having heard the man. Such speech-making I know *I'll* never hear again in this life."

"Ja, and since the two of you were so well acquainted and such good friends since childhood—" interrupted the bellringer in a malicious tone. His glance, traveling quickly from face to face in the little circle, showed he had relished the sweetness of the situation.

But the intoxication of victory was short-lived. The fact was, Nils had a sudden and violent temper. Now he was in the grip of it, and now it was time to make an "example" of Johnsgaard. And so it happened that before the latter could blink he found himself lying with his face to the floor. He fell so that it shook the building, and when he got up he was bleeding at the nose.

That it raised a big fuss was evident. The women were running around, moaning more loudly than the bellringer, and the minister came to see what was wrong. Nothing like this had happened before in the history of ladies' aid auctions.

"How was it that you could find it in yourself to strike your brother?" the minister said presently, turning to Nils.

"He is not, allow me to say, my brother," Nils snapped. "I would have the minister know that I come of honest folk."

"*Ja, ja*" said Nicolaisen, "that may very well be, but surely Nils is aware that we are all brothers in the Lord."

"Not with this one," answered Nils, "not me; I'll thank the minister not to say so.

"If I didn't know that you were a man of sobriety," the minister resumed after a bit, "I would have thought that you were inebriate."

Nils was still in a flying rage. He moved an inch closer to the minister, looked him in the face and asked:

"Does the minister say I'm drunk?"

Nicolaisen stepped back.

"*Nei, nei,* I said no such thing," he replied, "but you do you not realize, Nils, that you owe the congregation some explanation here?"

This Nils would not accept. It was no concern of the parish, he thought.

"If the minister had suffered as much disgrace in the congregation as I have," he said, "he'd boil over too once in awhile—if there's any warm blood in him, that is. If I can't even go to a meeting without hearing malicious words from such a ... such a ... such a deadbeat as that one there, so—*ja*, I almost said, then I might as well bid the minister goodbye."

Nicolaisen had to smile. He was not about to enter into further arguments.

Besides, it was seen that Johnsgaard had not been seriously injured in the conflict.

Now the auction got under way, and people were truly amazed: Nils was spending more money than he had spent at all of the previous ladies' aid auctions put together.

Next day, people saw Nils and Olava driving in their best clothes over to Johnsgaard's. As to what occured while they were there, one could only guess.

"Nils must be sorry that he called the bellringer a deadbeat." people said.

Whatever the case, there grew up an extraordinary friendship between the two families. And now whenever Nils talked about his trip to La Crosse there was no one to mix wormwood in the joy he still felt at being the only person in the settlement who had heard B.B.

ANNA BREKHUS NELSON

Solveig Nilsen

MY GRANDMOTHER, Anna Brekhus Nelson, was 95 when she died. Her death was expected, welcomed even, certainly not a tragedy. The days of her funeral became an unsought but cherished occasion for a gathering of the family, and a chance to tell, and re-tell, and embroider the family stories.

The day of the funeral I rode out to the Lake Preston Lutheran Church with my father and his sister and brother. I was to play the old pump organ at the funeral and needed time to practice. The three of them wanted, I think, some few moments together before the cousins and neighbors and friends arrived. In the car on the way out to the church, they told vivid tales, sharp, shorthand-like fragments of memories. I sat quietly, asking a question now and then, but mostly absorbing the sometimes poignant, sometime humorous stories. When we were almost there, when we could see the small country church on the horizon, they were silent for the first time. My father broke the silence, asking, "Did I ever tell you that Mother talked about the day of her mother's funeral on that tape I made with her over at Ebenezer two years ago?"

He promised to make copies to send to us. Three weeks later, when the tape arrived, I listened to my grandmother's amazingly unclouded memories of more than 80 years before. When the tape clicked off, I was dismayed to discover that the second side was blank, but astonished at the detail and power of the words that had been recorded. I offer here, without embroidery, Anna Brekhus' story of coming to the American plains from Norway.

You can't talk about it, she said. You just can't talk about it. But she talked anyway. On and on. How they had no land in the valley, just a small part of the mountain. Not so good for growing potatoes. In America, father said, you could get so much land, there'd be potatoes enough from one farm to feed all of Bergen. She told how father sold their part of that mountain in Voss, and used the money

47

it brought to buy 100 goats, which he butchered for sausage. The money he got from selling the goat sausage paid for the tickets to America. We sailed on a small boat from Voss to Bergen, she said, where we had to stay for a week before the big boat was ready to sail. You just can't imagine, she said, what this was like for us. We were thrilled: Bergen, staying in a real hotel! A couple days before we left mother took me aside, told me she'd heard stories of lice on the ship, and cut off my long red braids. Better short hair than lice-ridden braids. I was seven years old. It was my first haircut.

She told how mother had never wanted to leave Norway, how hard it was to feel her mother's sorrow at leaving her house, her frame house with a real basement, her valley in Voss. She told how two and a half years after arriving in the America she had no interest in seeing, far from her valley, her mountain, the sea. She died in childbed, in a sod house without windows, on the open prairie of South Dakota.

There was no question of having a doctor, she said. There was no doctor. But there hadn't even been a midwife. We didn't realize the child had been born until after we knew mother was dead. We didn't know, she said, because there was no birth-cry, no first gasp of breath. The child was still-born, as silent and lifeless as mother there on the bed. I remember how father hitched up the horses and drove the wagon to town for lumber, precious, expensive wood. Just think of it, she said, how he had to nail his wife's coffin together with his own hands, and then to pick up the unbaptised infant and place it in that fresh-made pine box together with his wife. I remember standing there by the side of the coffin. Mother was dressed in a white nightgown of fine batiste, embroidered, like a bride's gown.

She told of seeing father out by the shed, how she knew he'd wept before pulling himself together to return to the children, how terribly silent everyone was in their small dark sod house. I was only nine years old, but I knew that father's gruff manner was just his way of bearing it. She said. he would walk off away from us, from the house, and stand for a long time, his hands deep in the pockets of his overalls, staring across the prairie. I don't think he was seeing much, though, she said. Or nothing that was there, anyway. Norway maybe, Voss, the sea, his wife turned ghost. Maybe nothing. What can you see at a time like that?

Then the day of the funeral: I can see it all, just as clear, she said. The neighbor women came in the morning and twisted straw for the stove, baked spice cake for afterwards. There was no wood for the fire, you know; we burnt straw, or cornhusks, or dung. We went in the wagon to the cemetery. I remember everything. The horse, his name was Frank. We children loved that horse. There was no church yet, no minister even. It was 1894. She was the second person buried there, in the northwest corner of Lake Preston cemetary.

That next year father was out working by the week at hired jobs. We children were home by ourselves. We ate bread and milk, sometimes bread and sour cream with a bit of sugar sprinkled on it. You just can't talk about it, she said again, but after only a moment, went on. I remember late Saturday afternoons—that was when father would come back to us—Martha would sit on the grassy roof of the house (it wasn't so high you know) to be the first to see him coming from far off through the tall prairie grass. Red and I would sit at the corner, leaning against the sod wall of the house, waiting—Red hanging on my arm. One time I especially remember, Martha was crying up there on the roof; it was getting quite late and father still hadn't appeared on the horizon. I can just feel it, she said, that tight knot in my stomach when the clouds came in the northwest and father still wasn't home. Red—he was two then—would stick so close to me, hang on me.

Some neighbors wanted to adopt him, little Sivert the woman called him. We called him Red, for his hair, the same color as mine, as mother's. Father wouldn't hear of it. Red wasn't going to any neighbor, he said. But I was sent that year to work for Mrs. Braaten, to help with the new baby. I can tell you, I worked! But they were good to me. For the next five years I worked in people's homes, a hired girl. The year I was 13, father called me home. Time to "lese for presten," to read for the minister and make my confirmation. Every Saturday that year I walked seven miles to the church and seven miles home again. Plenty of time to think, she said, on those long walks over the fields to the church and back. Then the confirmation was over and I went away once more, hired girl again.

She started to tell what it was like, working out like that, but the tape stopped and the second side was blank. I wondered how long the conversation had gone on before my father remembered his intention to record it. I wondered about all the untold parts of her story. I promised myself to tell and tell and tell— all the stories I knew—hers, and mine, and ours.

KARL IVERSON

Rodney Nelson

Pain is sadness to one who has never been ill. For a young man it is an unnatural weight. But something has gone wrong in the stomach: this much has to be recognized. The pain began at horse-feeding time last night, then the snow, and there was little sleep. Now both the hut and the animal-shack are white up to the latches. One who chooses to homestead in Montana knows he has elected suffering, yet perhaps in his anticipation of brutal work he overlooks the spiritual hazard of coming out here, does not allow for the season's end, the tight companionless days with nothing to do but think, fear, turn heavy in the gut, and no one can afford to be ill in December. The horses will need their hay. They understand Norwegian.

Gudrun used to pass the cafe in Christiania every afternoon. The shipping company, her father's, occupied a large portion of the same block. Every other afternoon she would come in and join the intellectuals' table, where beauty and social position were all that a young woman of ordinary mental equipment needed to gain acceptance; yet she was not afraid of self-derision, and would lightly criticize *rich girls who not only stay home but work for their families as well.* Gudrun's laughter was unforgettable. Painter Munch, early a member of the table, had compared it to silver sunlight piercing the greens and greys of Christianian winter, and the poet Obstfelder was said to have loved her in girlhood for that quality alone, the shimmer of which had developed when she was still too young for men's eyes. It was remarkable how she never answered a question. A smile, a brief walk along the dripping storefronts of Karl Johan— these she could grant. But to the entreaties of a fosterchild with more half-brothers than brothers, a low-salaried intellectual who had missed knowing his peasant sire, Gudrun responded by turning to the next poor suitor at the table's far end, or, outside, to the hilarity of a fat banker trying to alight from his carriage, and there would be a raised cup, laughter, deafness. Perhaps she would have heard the less delicate tones of rich men, and to avoid these sought the company of the unformed but talented cafe-dwellers not yet established in her own high world. Winning Gudrun would have meant setting one's self up, planting a flag somewhere, at the least taking on an identity so that she could be free to laugh with one over the newspapers as she loved to do in the safely impersonal cafe, whether the item was Amundsen's latest polar brouhaha or the American railroads' trumpeting for settlers in Montana.

There's work to be had in the Valley, Karl; a strong man should have no trouble hiring on. But if it's land you want, the last chance is in the west. Half-brother Sigvart had been thirty years in America, and now the genius of the Norwegian tongue had deserted him. Except for a conservative few whom the great Hamsun might have understood, all of the prairie settlers spoke with the accent of red men, and listening to them was an exercise in patience. However, their wealth stood paramount in the visitor's mind. Had peasants ever dreamed of owning such an empire? Sigvart's farm, two hundred acres of black earth, was but one of countless others, equally huge, that occupied the Red River Valley; and from his porch one could see beyond the horizen, so strictly flat was the landscape. He talked of the *wheat boom,* of riches already banked, swearing that Canaan was no longer the exploitative fantasy of ministers—it had been realized through honest work. *This valley is the kingdom He promised us!* Gudrun should have been there. Half-brother Sigvart's claims were no less outrageous than the propaganda of James J. Hill in the advertisement she had read aloud for comic effect: *Lift up your eyes, O seeker: Eden awaits you! Oranges grow in this northwestern Paradise called Montana. Come now and take your share of a bounty exceeding that of that of North Dakota!* Yet a person might have stayed in the Valley. The Iversons—Sigvart mispelled the family name—held a picnic. All of the children sat quietly under the elms, and several neighbors were there, strapping peasants with wives and beautiful daughters; yet they were not the kind of people one met in Christiania. Two or three may have remembered Ibsen, but farmers soon forget. A person might have stayed, enjoying the serenity of an immigrant district where even the villages were called after Hedmark and Haugeby, luxuriating in a perhaps too earthbound way of life; and in 1911, who would be blamed for choosing it over the uncertainties of *the last chance?* Anyhow, Sigvart understood the beginning of the resolve: To have staked everything and come this far with the intention of establishing a place of one's own—

Winter hides the face of the land and covers the sky too, so that only the brown of the animal-shack relieves the whiteness. It was this they meant. *You don't want to go out in the autumn, Karl, it can get pretty rough by Thanksgiving.* But if not now, when? Fear had always existed: of leaving Christiania's narrow but secure haven, of the voyage, of landing among foreigners, of going it alone in a place where Europeans had never slept a night. The human spirit counterbalances fear, or makes use of it to further its will as on the morning when the train reached Hinsdale and Montana stretched out, pale and barren, in the early sunlight. At that moment, fear grew strong. What insanity had brought an educated man to renounce his proper destiny for that of a slave in the desert? There would be brutal work, isolation, unending contest with the elements, and at the fall of day, no soft Norwegian voices to console one. Fear takes the shape of doubt; but somehow the spirit was able to convert this into wild determination, and at once the homesteader was born. To hell with civilization! There has been enough culture! Take the plunge! If not here, where? After that, living became simple; a man exchanged his thoughts for nails, his dreams for horses, and prepared a shelter against whatever might come and drive him to it. Three hundred and twenty virgin acres awaited his plow in the Spring. Meanwhile, the light is diminishing, the birds are gone, it is hard to stand up.

Had there been a parting conversation on the dock or at the cafe entrance, Gudrun would have offered her smile as a gift for the journey: the emblem of all things left behind. That would have been a lover's farewell, old venturesome Norway saying goodbye again to the timeless Norway of the hearth, and her gift would have served as a charm for bold enterprise and safe return. It was raining as usual that spring night, the docks were crowded, and the traveler went on board alone. Gudrun had not a lover but lovers, each one denied the slightest intimacy. At the table, they expressed their hopes by nuance, and she affected to understand them literally. *Don't be too cruel, Gudrun; you might drive us to take ship for America, and how would you get along without entertainment?* Her reply caused general laughter: *Lift up your eyes, O seeker, Eden awaits you!* So there was no sharing of the plan, no warm conversation at the dock. A picture of her did remain, though not of the smile she would have reserved for one special person—it was of Gudrun pointing clownishly at the ceiling, her gold bracelet mirroring the lamplight. The ship moved out into the fjord, or was Christiania sailing away, Christiania where a young man could look forward to years of bachelorhood in a rented room? The town seemed reluctant to let go of this promise, to drift off into the rain not having grasped how the predetermined could ever be unfulfilled. It had all happened on the secret inspiration of wine; now she was gone, and one would have to find riches to lure her back.

James J. Hill's iron path to Paradise bent westward at Grand Forks, having toured the fields of the Valley. On the seat there was a straw basket which Sigvart's wife had packed with food, but he himself had inserted a bottle of American liquor. *You might have trouble sleeping on the long ride.* Others were pursuing the dream as well, and the coach was full of quiet men in dirty chambray; one overheard remarks in English, Swedish, German and various dialects of the mother tongue, but for the most part they silently watched the passage of the landscape. The basket also contained an issue of *Red River Posten*, and behind the shield of this newspaper one could enjoy a nip without offending the passengers. However, by the time the train stopped at Rugby, every second man was displaying a paper of his own. *Good luck, Karl. To tell the truth, I wish I could go along and start all over again. They say you get twice as much land in Montana. But an older man has to be thankful for what he has already gotten.* There were few hills now, and a steady yellowing of the prairie. Drink kept the fear in abeyance as the train rocked through the night which was to become almost impossible to recall. The memories of one's drunken episodes are like those of early childhood, fragmentary and grotesque; to interpret them one must uncork the bottle again, or perhaps the names of *Minot* and *Williston* belonged to a time as much beyond recapture as infancy. By contrast, how vivid the sailing from Christiania and the arrival at Hinsdale, Montana: these moments seemed eternal. A person might have experienced them before they happened. Of that strange night journey, the only thing to survive was a sensation of acting contrary to instinct, committing a fundamental error.

No one can afford to be ill in December, so one takes care beforehand. Supplies are laid in, the hut secured, regular contact with a neighbor maintained. Letters make an excellent bulwark against loneliness, therefore one tends to the correspondence. But suppose the neighbor gives up his claim and it is five miles to the next homestead, and a winter storm abruptly cuts one off from civilization? Then illness means heavy expense. Sigvart's last letter is on the table. *I hope you are managing well in that remote country. It's not good to be altogether alone, particularly at Christmas, so maybe you could spend the holidays here. Anyway, I am sending you a box of wool clothes. I almost forgot to mention that I heard from our sister Anna in Norway. She says that a fellow in Christiania wanted to talk to you about some financial irregularity at the office where you used to clerk. I guess they are checking with everyone. Evidently the amount was not considerable, so I don't why the bother after all this time. If there's anything we can do for you, Karl, you have only to ask.* Every man is allowed a number of mistakes; exceed it, and the entire weight of them gathers in the stomach to cleanse by destroying. Perhaps the one who creates omens for men to see and read cannot tolerate too much willful blindness. In that light, the pain is just. Snow falls and falls on the vacant land which will remain here whether people do or not. The horses are probably comfortable in their shack; but soon they'll be fed, chided in Norwegian for the last time, and turned loose.

ZACHAEUS

Knut Hamsun

KNUT HAMSUN (1859-1952) worked as a farmhand in the Red River valley during the 1880's and it is probably that experience that suggested the general scenario for the following story, which has been translated from the Norwegian by Sverre Arestad, emeritus professor of Scandinavian languages and comparative literature at the University of Washington, Seattle.

Hamsun, who won the Nobel Prize in 1920, might be accused of writing an anti-Irish story in "Zachaeus," but the human characters are not really the most important. The most powerful presence in the story—at its beginning and end—is the prairie itself, which makes all men seem petty and insignificant. In novels like Growth of the Soul *(1917) Hamsun revealed a mystical love of the land itself and its transcendence of feeble and "civilized" humanity.*

According to one legend (and there are many) Hamsun lost his job as a streetcar conductor in Chicago because his supervisor found him reading Euripides on the rear platform and missing his stops. The incident—true or apocryphal—reveals, as does "Zachaeus," Hamsun's droll sense of humor and delight in the incongruous.

The prairie rests in the deepest peace. For miles there are no trees and no houses to see, just wheat and green grass as far as the eye can reach. Far, far away, as small as flies, horses and people can be seen at work; it is the haying hands sitting on their machines mowing. The only audible sound is the chirp of the grasshoppers, and when there is a current of air toward us once in a great while, the staccato buzz of the mowing machines down on the horizon. At times this noise sounds strangely near.

55

The place is the Billybony Farm. It lies absolutely alone in the wide West, without neighbors, without connection with the world, and the nearest little prairie town is several days' march away. At a distance the buildings on the farm look like a couple of tiny skerries in the endless sea of wheat. No one lives on the farm in winter; but from spring until late in October seventy-odd men are at work with the wheat. There are three men in the kitchen, the cook and his two helpers, and there are twenty mules in the stable in addition to the many horses, but no women, not a single woman on Billybony Farm.

The sun bakes at 102 degrees Fahrenheit, the sky and the earth vibrate in this heat, and no breeze cools the air. The sun looks like a morass of fire.

Everything is quiet at home by the buildings, but from the large, shingled shed that is used for a kitchen and dining room one hears the voice and the steps of the cook and his helpers who are rushing about in bustling activity. They burn grass in the huge stoves, and the smoke that wells up out of the chimney is mixed with sparks and flames. When the food is ready, it is carried out in zinc tubs and loaded on wagons. Then the mules are hitched up, and the three men haul the food out on the prairie.

The cook is a huge Irishman, forty years old, gray-haired, with a military appearance. He is half naked, his shirt is open, and his chest is like a millstone. Everyone called him "Polly" because his face resembles that of a parrot.

Polly has been a soldier, stationed at one of the forts in the South; he is literary and can read. Therefore he has a song book along at the farm and besides that an old copy of a newspaper. He permits none of the people to touch these treasures; he has them lying on a shelf in the kitchen in order to have them at hand in free moments. And he makes diligent use of them.

But Zachaeus, his miserable countryman, who is almost blind and uses glasses, once took the newspaper to read it. It did no good to offer Zachaeus an ordinary book whose small letters rose in a fog before his eyes; on the other hand it was a real pleasure to hold the cook's newspaper in his hands and loiter over the big letters of the advertisements. But the cook immediately missed his treasure, sought Zachaeus in his bed and tore the newspaper out of his hands. Then a violent, droll wrangling arose between these two men.

The cook called Zachaeus a black-hearted bandit and a son of a bitch. He snapped his fingers under his nose and asked him if he had ever been a soldier and if he knew how a fort is outfitted. No, well! Then he had better look out, look out, by God. Shut up! How much did he earn a month? Did he own property in Washington and did his cow calve yesterday?

Zachaeus made no answer to that, but he accused the cook of not cooking the food until done and serving bread pudding with flies in it. "Go to hell and take your newspaper with you!" He—Zachaeus—was an honest man; he would have put the newspaper back when he had studied it. "Don't stand there and spit on the floor, you dirty dog!"

And Zachaeus' blind eyes stood like two hard steel balls in his raging face.

But from that day on there was eternal enmity between those two countrymen.

The wagons with the food spread out over the prairie, and each feeds twenty-seven men. The people come running from all directions, grab some food, and throw themselves under the wagons and the mules to get some shade during meal time. In ten minutes the food is eaten. The foreman is already in the saddle, ordering the people back to work again, and the chuck wagons drive back to the farm.

But while the cook's helpers wash the dishes and pots and pans from the noonday meal, Polly himself sits in the shade behind the house reading for the thousandth time his songs and soldiers' ballads in his precious book, which he had brought along from the fort in the South. Then Polly is a soldier again.

In the evening, when twilight already has fallen, seven hay wagons roll slowly homeward with the hired men. Most of them wash their hands out in the yard before they go in to supper, some also comb their hair. There are people of all nations and several races, there are younger people and older ones, immigrants from Europe and native-born American vagabonds, all of them more or less infamous wretches and "derailed existences."

The more prosperous of the gang carry revolvers in their hip pockets. The food is usually eaten in all haste, without anyone saying much of anything. These people have respect for the foreman who eats with them and keeps an eye on things. When the meal is over, the men immediately go to rest.

But now Zachaeus was going to wash his shirt. It had got so hard from sweat that it chafed him during the day when the sun roasted his back.

Zachaeus went over to the kitchen wall where several containers of rain water stood. It was the cook's water; he collected it carefully on rainy days because the water on Billybony Farm was too hard and alkaline to wash with. Zachaeus took possession of one of the containers, removed his shirt and began to rub it. The evening was quiet and cold; he froze terribly, but his shirt had to be washed and he even whistled a bit to stiffen himself up.

Then the cook suddenly opened the kitchen door. He held a lamp in his hand and a broad beam of light fell on Zachaeus.

"Aha!" said the cook and stepped out.

He set the lamp down on the kitchen steps, went right up to Zachaeus and asked "Who has given you that water?"

"I took it," answered Zachaeus.

"It's my water!" shouted Polly. "You've taken it, you slave, you liar, thief, son of a bitch!"

Zachaeus gave no particular answer to this; he just began to repeat the accusation about the flies in the pudding.

The commotion from the two fellows brought the men from the bunkhouse. They stood there in groups freezing, listening with the greatest attention to the exchange of words.

"Isn't this great of the little swine? My own water?" Polly shouted at them.

"Take your water!" said Zachaeus and emptied the container. "I'm through with it."

"Did you see that?" asked the cook as he thrust his fist under his nose.

"Yes," answered Zachaeus.

"I'll give you a taste of it."

"If you dare."

Then suddenly the sound of rapid blows being exchanged was heard. The onlookers emitted howl after howl as an expression of their applause and good spirits.

But Zachaeus did not last long. The blind, stocky Irishman was as desperate as a Lapland marmot, but his arms were far too short to be at all effective against the cook. Finally he reeled sideways three, four steps over the yard and fell down.

"Well, there he lies. Let him lie, a soldier has felled him," the cook said as he turned toward the crowd.

"I think he is dead," said a voice.

The cook shrugged his shoulders.

"Very, well!" he answered overweeningly. And he felt like a great, conquering victor before the people. He threw back his head and waited to underscore his respect; he became literary.

"To devil with him," he said, "let him lie. Is he the American Daniel Webster? Here he comes and wants to teach me how to bake pudding, I who have cooked for generals! Is he the Colonel of the Prairie, I ask you?"

And everyone admired Polly's speech.

Then Zachaeus got up from the ground and said just as inveterately, just as defiantly: "Come on, you coward!"

The men bellowed ecstatically; but the cook smiled pityingly and answered: "Nonsense! I might as well fight with this lamp."

Thereupon he took the lamp and stalked slowly in.

Darkness fell on the yard, and the men returned to the bunkhouse. Zachaeus picked up his shirt, wrung it out carefully and put it on. Then he too sauntered after the others to find his bunk and go to bed.

The next day Zachaeus knelt in the grass out on the prairie oiling his machine. The sun was just as severe today, and his eyes ran full of sweat behind his glasses. Suddenly the horses jerked forward a couple of steps; either they had been frightened by something or insects had stung them. Zachaeus emitted a shriek and jumped high off the ground. Shortly after he began to swing his hand in the air and pace back and forth with hurried steps.

A man who was raking a distance away stopped his horses and asked: "What's the matter?"

"Come over here a minute and help me."

When the man came up to him Zachaeus showed him a bloody hand and said, "One of my fingers has been cut off; it just happened. Hunt for the finger, I can't see."

The man hunted for the finger and found it in the grass. There were two joints. They were already beginning to wither and looked like a little corpse.

Zachaeus took the finger in his hand, recognized it and remarked: "Yes, that's it. Wait a moment, hold it a second."

He pulled out his shirt tail and tore two strips off it; with the one he bandaged his hand, in the other he wrapped his amputated finger and put in his pocket. Then he thanked his comrade for his help and got up on his machine again.

He held out almost to suppertime. When the foreman heard of his misfortune, he bawled him out and sent him home to the farm at once.

The first thing Zachaeus did was to hide his amputated finger. He had no alcohol, so he poured machine oil into a bottle, dropped the finger in it and corked it. He put the finger under the straw mattress in his bunk.

He stayed home a whole week. He got violent pains in his hand and had to lie absolutely still night and day. It affected his head, and he also got fever in his body, and he suffered and complained excessively. He had never before experienced an inactivity of this nature, not even the time some years ago when a mine blast went off and injured his eyes.

To make his miserable condition still worse, Polly the cook himself brought the food every day to his bed and used the opportunity to provoke the wounded man. The two enemies had many a nasty quarrel during this time, and it happened more than once that Zachaeus had to turn to the wall and clench his teeth in silence because he was powerless before the giant.

However, the painful days and nights continued to go and come, to go and come again with unendurable slowness. As soon as possible, Zachaeus began to sit up in his bunk a little, and during the heat of the day he had the door open to the prairie and the sky. Often he sat with open mouth listening for the sound of the mowing machines far, far away, and then he spoke aloud to his horses as though he had them at hand.

But the malicious, wily Polly would not leave him in peace. He came and closed the door on the pretense that there was a draft, that there was a terrible draft, and he must not expose himself to a draft. Beside himself, Zachaeus tumbled out of his bunk and sent a shoe or a stool after the cook, vowing to cripple him for life. But Zachaeus had no luck; he saw too poorly to be able to aim, and he never hit his mark.

The seventh day he announced that he wanted to eat dinner in the kitchen. The cook told him that he simply didn't want him to come. That settled it, Zachaeus had to eat his food in his bunk that day too. He sat there completely forlorn, in agonized boredom. Now he knew that the kitchen was empty. The cook and his helpers were out on the prairie with the noonday meal. He heard them depart, laughing and shouting, exulting over the shut-in.

Zachaeus got out of his bunk and staggered over to the kitchen. He looked about. The book and the newspaper were lying in their place. He seized the newspaper and stumbled back to the bunkhouse. Then he wiped his glasses and began to read the pleasingly large letters of the advertisements.

An hour passed, two hours—the hours passed so rapidly now. Zachaeus finally heard the chuck wagons returning and he heard the cook's voice as usual ordering the helpers to wash the dishes and the pots and pans.

Zachaeus knew that the newspaper would be missed, because, as was his custom, the cook would go to his library now. He thought a moment and stuck the newspaper under the straw mattress in his bunk. After a bit, he quickly removed the newspaper and put it inside his shirt. He would never give it up again!

A minute passed.

Then the heavy steps approached the bunkhouse where Zachaeus lay staring at the ceiling.

Polly entered.

"How about it? You got my newspaper?" he asked and stopped in the middle of the floor.

"No," answered Zachaeus.

"You've got it." hissed the cook and stepped nearer to him.

Zachaeus got up.

"I don't have your newspaper. Go to hell!" he said, infuriated.

At that the cook threw the sick man onto the floor and began to hunt in the bunk. He turned the straw mattress over and searched the miserable quilt several times without finding what he sought.

"You've got it," he continued. Then he left, but when he had come clear out in the yard he turned and repeated: "You have taken it. But you just wait!"

Then Zachaeus laughed delightedly and mischievously and said "All right, I've taken it. I had use for it, you dirty swine."

The cook's parrot face turned blood red, and an ill-boding expression came into his villainous eyes. He looked back at Zachaeus and mumbled: "Just wait!"

There was stormy weather the next day, rain, violent streams of water that struck against the houses like hail showers and soon filled the cook's containers early in the morning. The whole crew was inside, some were patching wheat sacks for fall, others were repairing tools and sharpening sickles.

When the call for the noonday meal sounded, Zachaeus rose from his bunk to follow the others into the dining room. He was met outside the door by Polly, however, who was bringing him his food. Zachaeus objected that he had decided to eat with the others from now on, his hand was better, and he did not have any more fever. The cook answered that if he didn't want the food that was brought to him, he wouldn't get any. He threw the tin dish into Zachaeus' bunk and asked, "Perhaps that isn't good enough for you?"

Zachaeus, resigned, returned to his bunk. It was best to take the food he got.

"What kind of pig feed is this that you have cooked today?" he grumbled, and busied himself with the dish.

"Spring chicken," answered the cook. And a strange glint came into his eye as he turned and went out.

"Spring chicken?" Zachaeus mumbled to himself and searched the food thoroughly with his blind eyes. "The devil it is, you liar! But it is meat and gravy."

And he ate of the meat.

All at once he got a piece in his mouth that he couldn't identify. He couldn't cut it, it was a bone with tough meat on it, and when he had gnawed one side of it, he took it out of his mouth and looked at it. "That dog can keep his bone himself," he mumbled and walked over to the door to examine it more carefully. He turned and twisted it about several times. Suddenly he hurried back to his bunk and looked for the bottle with the amputated finger. The bottle was there, but the finger was gone.

Zachaeus walked over to the dining room. He stopped inside the door, pale as death, his face distorted, and as he held something up, he asked the cook so everyone heard it: "Hey, Polly, isn't this my finger?"

The cook didn't answer, but began to titter over at his table.

Zachaeus held something else up and asked:"And, Polly, isn't this the nail that was on my finger? Don't you think I recognize it?"

Now all the men became aware of Zachaeus' strange questions and looked at him in amazement.

"What's wrong with you?" someone asked.

"I found my finger, my amputated finger, in my food," explained Zachaeus. "He cooked it and served it to me in my food. Here is the fingernail, too."

Then suddenly a roar of laughter burst from all the tables and everyone shouted at once. "Did he cook your own finger and serve it to you? And I see you've bit into it, you've gnawed off the meat on one side."

"I don't see well," answered Zachaeus, "I didn't know ... didn't think ...

Then all at once he was silent, turned and walked out of the door again.

The foreman had to restore order in the dining room. He got up, turned to the cook and asked: "Did you cook the finger with the other meat, Polly?"

"No,"answered Polly. "Good God, no. What do you take me for? I cooked it separately in an entirely different pot."

The story of the cooked finger became a source of inexhaustible pleasure for the gang the whole afternoon. People discussed it and laughed over it like lunatics, and the cook had won triumph as never before in his life. But Zachaeus had disappeared.

Zachaeus had gone out on the prairie. The storm continued, and there wasn't a shelter anywhere; but Zachaeus wandered farther and farther out over the prairie. His sore hand was bandaged and he protected it as well as he could from the rain; otherwise he was soaked through from head to foot.

He continued to walk. When twilight began to fall he stopped, looked at his watch by the glare of a flash of lightning, then returned the same way he had come. He walked with heavy, deliberate steps through the wheat as though had had calculated the time and his speed carefully. Around eight o'clock he was home at the farm again.

It was now absolutely dark. He hears that the men are eating supper in the dining room, and as he peeks in through the window he thinks he sees the cook there and that he is in good humor.

He walks away from the house, over to the stable where he gets under cover and stares into the darkness. The grasshoppers are silent, everything is quiet, but the rain falling and now and then a sulpher-colored flash of lightning splits the sky and strikes down far out on the prairie.

Finally he hears that the men are coming from the supper and setting out for the bunkhouse, swearing, and running so as not to get wet. Zachaeus still waits an hour or so, patiently and doggedly, then he proceeds toward the kitchen.

It is still light in there; he sees a man by the stove and he walks calmly in.

"Good evening," he greets.

The cook looks surprised at him and finally says: "You can't have any food tonight."

Zachaeus answers: "Good, but give me a little soap, Polly. I didn't get my shirt clean last night, I have to wash it again."

"Not in my water," says the cook.

"Yes, exactly. I have it around the corner."

"I advise you not to do it."

"Do I get soap?" asks Zachaeus.

"I'll give you soap," answers the cook. "Get out!" And Zachaeus goes out.

He takes one of the containers, carries it over to the corner right under the kitchen window and begins to splash vigorously in the water. The cook hears it and goes out.

Today he feels superior as never before and he goes right toward Zachaeus with rolled up sleeves, determined and angry.

"What are you doing?" he asks.

"Nothing," Zachaeus answers. "Just washing my shirt."

"In my water?"

"Of course."'

The cook comes closer, leans over the container to identify it and feels in the water for the shirt.

Then Zachaeus draws his revolver out of the bandage on his sore hand, thrusts it right into the cook's ear and pulls the trigger.

A dull report sounds in the wet night.

When Zachaeus late at night came into the bunkhouse to go to bed, a couple of fellows woke up. They asked what he had been doing out so long.

"Nothing," answered Zachaeus. "By the way, I have shot Polly."

The fellows got up on their elbows in order to hear better.

"You have shot him?"

"Yes."

"The devil you say! Where did you hit him?"

"In the head. I shot him through the ear, upward."

"I'll be damned! Where did you bury him?"

"Out west on the prairie. I laid the newspaper between his hands."

"You did?"

Then the fellows lie down to sleep again.

A while later one of them asks: "Did he die right away?"

"Yes," answered Zachaeus, "almost immediately. The bullet went right through his brain."

"Yes, that's the best shot," the fellow agrees. "If the bullet goes through the brain, it is death."

Then it becomes quiet in the bunkhouse and everyone sleeps.

The next day the foreman had to appoint a new cook, one of the old helpers who now rose to chef and was exceedingly happy about the murder.

Everything went its wonted way until fall. Not much was said about Polly's departure, the poor devil lay buried in the wheatland some place where the wheat was torn up. There was nothing more to do about that.

When October came, Billybony's workers proceeded to the nearest town to drink a farewell with one another and separate. All were at this moment better friends than ever, and they embraced one another and set them up for one another in good spirit.

"Where are you going, Zachaeus?"

"A little farther west," answered Zachaeus. "To Wyoming perhaps. But when winter comes, I'll head for the lumber camps again."

"Then we'll meet there. So-long for now, Zachaeus. Have a good trip."

And the fellows take off in all directions out into the immense Yankeeland. Zachaeus is going to Wyoming.

And the prairie remains behind as an endless sea over which the October sun shines with long beams that look like awls.

II. VOICES FROM THE IMMIGRANT TRUNK: A SAMPLER OF FOLK TALES BROUGHT TO THE NEW WORLD

THE FOLLOWING TALES are just a few of those brought by Norwegian immigrants to the New World in both written and oral form. Although the tales are set in Norway and have the timeless quality of stories that are part of an oral tradition, each has "transport" value and each suggests values and personal qualities which are "useful" in the New World.

Folklore tends to be an "unofficial" or "non-institutional" part of a culture and presents an "unofficial" and often ironic perception of that culture. Often a "trickster" figures—clever in deed and word—is present and manages to practice his one-upmanship against a scenario of "official" reality. The New World legend for the first two of the tales might well be, "It pays to be tricky in a new country." Of course, frugal, hard-working Norwegians might resent the legend, but "tricky" might simply be interpreted to mean "clever" or "enterprising" and that, after all, was what success was much about in the New World. If America had its Ben Franklin and Horatio Alger, Norway had its own mythology of "getting ahead"—especially in the Askelad, a hybridization of the hard-working Norwegian boy and the clever Loki of Norse mythology. And the Askelad was ready to strive and succeed in any scenario—from Bergen to St. Paul.

THREE OLD NORSE FAIRY STORIES

Contributed by Helen M. Lynch

Mrs. Helen Lynch, who made the following three tales available for this anthology, notes that the first was told to her by her grandmother. The second and thrid stories, TORGER and IMAGINATION, were told to her by an old Lutheran minister who lived next door to Mrs. Lynch during her childhood in North Dakota.

1. FRITZ THE DUMBLING

The sleigh bells jingled merrily that bright winter day as the two aging subjects of the well-loved old King stood gazing up at the balconies of the winter palace.

Hans Neilson squinted his blue eyes against the sun's glare as he spoke. "Ya, I hear that our good King is giving up the throne, and I suppose that means that young Fritz will soon wear the crown." He shook his head sorrowfully. "It is a shame that the crown goes to the eldest boy—one of the twins would be better. I don't know about that Fritz—he is peculiar—that one."

"Fritz, the Dumbling, you mean," Ole Hagen corrected him, laughing. "I would rather be ruled by my dog Fisk than by Fritz. Fisk, I think, is smarter."

"Ya, one of the twins should get it."

"But they both drink too much wine—those two."

"Ah, so did we when we were young, but we soon settled down and so will they."

"I don't know—I don't know. It is a bad choice for Norway—a stupid king or a wine drinker." The two old men shook their heads sadly.

Up in the winter palace, the King's oldest advisers waited for him to speak. "My friends," he said, "I have grown old and I wish to pass on the throne to my son. It is right that Fritz, my first born, should wear the crown."

The oldest of all the advisers spoke slowly. "My King, I ask your forgiveness, but I feel I should say this. We are of one mind here; we do not think that Fritz will make Norway a suitable ruler. He is not well-understood by the people."

The old King smiled sadly. "You mean that he is not well-thought of. I know what they call him. 'Fritz—Fritz, the Dumbling' It has come to my ears. But my Fritz is not stupid, my friends. He only dreams much. I have faith in Fritz, but since you don't, I will put my three boys to a test, and the one that comes out the best—that one will be the King of Norway. Such a way is fair. If Fritz proves himself foolish, then one of the twins will be crowned. Is it agreed?"

The King's friends nodded, and they smiled to themselves. Now they knew that Norway would soon be ruled by one of the younger boys. Fritz would never wear the crown of Norway.

The next morning the three boys stood before their father. "I am old," he said. "I wish to leave the throne to one of you, and I have devised a test to determine which one of you deserves such an honor. Each one of you will be given 3000 kroner and a horse. You are to leave the palace and return in a week. The one who has handled his wealth the wisest will be king." He held out the bags of gold which the twins grabbed up, eager to be away. But Fritz refused his share.

"Father, I do not wish the gold. I want a knapsack, a ball of cottage cheese wrapped up in a cheese cloth, and a huge packet of bird seed. I won't need a horse because I shall go up above the fjords into the mountains."

"Son, son," the old King urged softly, "take the gold and the horse. You must not go up there alone where only the trolls live. They will surely kill you."

"No, father, I must go where my heart tells me to go. You have forgotten the little folk—they are my friends. They live there too. Don't look so sad, Father."

"Oh, my dear son, I wish you would change your plans," the old man pled earnestly, but Fritz only shook his head.

"Don't worry, father. I will be all right," Fritz assured him.

The three brothers left the palace together, but soon Fritz waved to them and turned off on a small trail that led up the side of the mountains. He traveled all day and the snow became very deep. Just as the sun was setting, he stopped to look about for a place to spend the night. It was bitter cold. Suddenly he heard the sound of thousands of birds all chirping in a pitiful chorus.

"Poor creatures. They sound like they are in trouble," he said aloud. Then looking down, he saw a small nissen in a red-tasseled cap and turned-up green shoes. "Would you know what is wrong with the birds?" Fritz asked the little man.

"They are starving," he answered. "The snow is too deep for them to scratch seeds. Come, I'll show you."

Fritz followed the little fellow and found hundreds of birds crumpled on the snow. "How horrible," Fritz said. "I can help them though. Help me spread my seeds."

They threw the seeds over the snowy crust, and the birds began to eat, but now it was almost dark, and Fritz's small friend had disappeared. Fritz leaned his back against a tree when suddenly the tree moved. Startled, he looked up to find a vicious, bearded old troll grinning down at him.

"Well, little man," the troll growled, "I am glad that you found me. I am hungry for meat tonight, and you will make me a fine supper."

"Oh, Mr. Troll, but you are mistaken. You wouldn't enjoy eating me at all.

My flesh would be too tough and stringy. You see, I am the strongest man in the world."

The troll threw back his head and laughed until the tears ran down into his bushy moustache. "Don't tell me jokes. I am the strongest. You are only a little man."

"If you are so strong, can you squeeze water out of a stone? I can, you see."

The troll stopped laughing. "Let's see what you can do, little man."

Fritz leaned over and picked up a round white rock and dropped it in his knapsack. but there he exchanged it for his ball of cottage cheese. He brought out the cheese and squeezed it until a little trickle of whey-water dripped into the snow.

"Give me that rock, little man," the troll cried in astonishment.

Fritz quickly exchanged the rock for the cheese inside his knapsack, and the troll squeezed the rock until his eyes popped. "Do it again, little man," he begged, handing Fritz the stone. Fritz slipped the stone into his knapsack and brought out the cheese. Again the watery whey dribbled down.

After struggling one more time to squeeze the rock, the troll tossed it angrily into a snowbank. "Well, little man," he grumbled ill-temperedly, "you may be stronger than I, but I can cut down more trees than you. You come home with me tonight. Tomorrow we will chop down trees. If I can cut more than you, then I shall have you for my dinner."

The next morning Fritz chose the troll's lightest axe which he could barely lift, and they set off for a nearby mountain that had never been logged.

"You take this side, and I'll take the other," the troll ordered. "At sundown, we shall see who cut the most logs," and the troll strode off to his side of the mountain.

By mid-morning, Fritz hands were bleeding and he had felled his first tree. When he sat down to rest, he heard the crashing of the trees that the troll was felling. Discouraged, he nearly wept with fear and weariness. But suddenly he found his little nissen friend peering up at him.

"What's the matter, Fritz? Why are you so sad?"

"Oh, kind friend, I think this is the end of me. I have met a troll, and he forced me into a tree-cutting contest. Listen to his trees falling! If I don't cut more than he does, he will kill me. I am surely lost this time."

"Oh, no. Just a minute. You wait here. I think I have the answer to your problems." The little fellow waved happily at Fritz and disappeared.

Only moments later, Fritz saw that the sky was alive with birds. Each bird chose a tree and began pecking rapidly. "Rat-a-tat-tat! Rat-a-tat-tat!" was the sound that came from every direction as the trees began falling.

"What are they doing, little friend?" Fritz yelled excitedly.

"Those are the wood peckers you fed. You saved them and now they will save you."

Fritz threw back his head and gave a joyous laugh as the trees fell. When the troll arrived, the big fellow stopped in disbelief when he saw the bare mountain.

mush equally. "You, little man, you eat on your side and I'll eat mine. The one that eats the most is the winner." The troll began to scoop up the mush.

Fritz took several mouthfuls of the stuff, and gave up, but the troll ate on, never raising his eyes. Seeing this, Fritz opened the top of his knapsack that hung about his neck and began shoving great slabs of the mush into his sack. Faster and faster he scooped, always keeping an eye on the troll to see that he did not look up and catch him. Finally the troll raised his eyes in astonishment.

"Little man, how do you do it? You are such a little man!"

"It is a secret," Fritz answered him pleasantly.

"Teach me that secret," the troll begged.

"Put your head under the table then, and I'll show you. Now do you see my fat stomach resting on my knees?" Fritz patted the fat knapsack full of mush. "Now look here, Mr. Troll. When I get full, I just take my hunting knife so and run it into the bottom of my stomach and rip it across and all the mush runs out. Now look up. See, the mush is on the floor and I am ready to eat again."

"Give me that knife," the troll roared excitedly. Fritz happily handed him the knife, and after a terrible groan, the troll dropped down dead beneath the table.

Then Fritz toured the house. He found long tunnels of gold which the troll had hoarded. Why, this old scoundrel is unbelievably rich," Fritz said happily. "How pleased my father will be, for I shall now claim this and I am rich!"

The next morning, he arrived home to find that the twins were there before him with their kroners spent, but when Fritz saw his father, he handed him a handful of gold from his pocket. "Father," he said, "this is only a sampling. There is so much gold there that Norway can live in prosperity for many years."

"Little man, how did you do it?" he asked, but Fritz only laughed.

But now the troll's eyes grew cunning. "Little man, you may be strong enough to squeeze stones and cut logs, but I can eat more than you. You come home with me. If you can't beat me, then that will be the end of you!"

So Fritz went home once again with the troll where the big fellow cooked a huge flat pan of mush—so large that it covered the whole table top. With his hunting knife, the troll drew a line through the middle of the pan, dividing the

The old King's eyes grew warm with pride. "You have done well, my son, as I knew you would. I am pleased to leave our beloved country in your hands. Tomorrow, Fritz, you shall receive the crown."

The next day, Fritz was crowned King of Norway, and he ruled with kindness and generosity for seventy years.

"Little man, how did you do it?" he asked, but Fritz only laughed.

But now the troll's eyes grew cunning. "Little man, you may be strong enough to squeeze stones and cut logs, but I can eat more than you. You come home with me. If you can't beat me, then that will be the end of you!"

So Fritz went home once again with the troll where the big fellow cooked a huge flat pan of mush—so large that it covered the whole table top. With his hunting knife, the troll drew a line through the middle of the pan, dividing the mush equally. "You, little man, you eat on your side and I'll eat mine. The one that eats the most is the winner." The troll began to scoop up the mush.

Fritz took several mouthfuls of the stuff, and gave up, but the troll ate on, never raising his eyes. Seeing this, Fritz opened the top of his knapsack that hung about his neck and began shoving great slabs of the mush into his sack. Faster and faster he scooped, always keeping an eye on the troll to see that he did not look up and catch him. Finally the troll raised his eyes in astonishment.

"Little man, how do you do it? You are such a little man!"

"It is a secret," Fritz answered him pleasantly.

"Teach me that secret," the troll begged.

"Put your head under the table then, and I'll show you. Now do you see my fat stomach resting on my knees?" Fritz patted the fat knapsack full of mush. "Now look here, Mr. Troll. When I get full, I just take my hunting knife so and run it into the bottom of my stomach and rip it across and all the mush runs out. Now look up. See, the mush is on the floor and I am ready to eat again."

"Give me that knife," the troll roared excitedly. Fritz happily handed him the knife, and after a terrible groan, the troll dropped down dead beneath the table.

Then Fritz toured the house. He found long tunnels of gold which the troll had hoarded. Why, this old scoundrel is unbelievably rich," Fritz said happily. "How pleased my father will be, for I shall now claim this and I am rich!"

The next morning, he arrived home to find that the twins were there before him with their kroners spent, but when Fritz saw his father, he handed him a handful of gold from his pocket. "Father," he said, "this is only a sampling. There is so much gold there that Norway can live in prosperity for many years."

The old King's eyes grew warm with pride. "You have done well, my son, as I knew you would. I am pleased to leave our beloved country in your hands. Tomorrow, Fritz, you shall receive the crown."

The next day, Fritz was crowned King of Norway, and he ruled with kindness and generosity for seventy years.

corrected page

2. TORGER

Torger was angry. It was not his usual under-the-surface, simmering annoyance with his wife Bergit—he simply exploded. It occurred over such a little thing as a button she had replaced on his coat.

"I have stood enough!" he roared. "Why—why do I of all men have such a stupid wife? Why can't you be like other wives—thrifty, and—and normal? But, no! Last week it was the cheese you ruined! The week before you made a shirt for me that was only big enough for a child. And now this!" He looked down at the gaping bulge just at his waist-line where the button was attached too high, making one side of his coat short, and producing this horrible bulge.

"But I do try, Torger. I do!" she cried. "Can I help it if I am not clever with a needle?"

"It isn't just a needle," he shouted. "It is everything you do. You have to be the stupidest woman in all of Norway. I can't stand it anymore! I won't live under the same roof with you any longer. It is too much! I shall—I shall"—he looked down wordlessly at his gaping coat—"I shall leave, and I shall never come back!" Now it was out! Now he had said it! And he would go.

Wild-eyed, she ran to him and pressed her weeping face against the rough coat. "But Torger, you can't leave me. I love you, Torger."

"But I am going. Take your arms away. Tears will not help this time. You are the stupidest woman in all of Norway! Now let me go."

But still she clung, weeping bitterly. "But Torger, there must be more foolish women than I am. You are not fair to me."

"There are not! There couldn't be! You are the worst. Let me go." He tried to unwind her arms from about his neck.

"Torger, listen to me. I know I am stupid, and I know you will leave me if you say you will. I am sure I deserve it—but Torger, will you promise me one thing? If ever you find three women in Norway more foolish than I—will you then come home to me again?"

He looked down into her anxious, tear-stained face. She was a pretty little thing. Then he sighed heavily. Unlocking her arms, he set her back from him. "Yes, yes. I guess I am safe in promising you that. There will never be three as stupid as you—I know that. And now I will leave." He tore off the offending button and threw it into the corner. Now his coat hung properly, at least. Then he strode out into the spring sunshine without a backward look at her sad little face. His mind was made up.

As he walked along the country road, he reviewed ruefully his short years with Bergit. Everything had gone wrong right from the start. She couldn't cook she couldn't sew, and her knitting was a mass of tangles which she never finished.

72

She was wasteful. He shook his head. Surely the best place for him was as far away from her as he could get.

Toward evening he was astonished to hear a loud wailing coming from the other side of a small hill. Rounding the curve, he stopped short in amazement, for there, tied to the chimney on top of a sod-roofed house hung a rope, and on the end of the rope dangled a dead cow. Below the cow stood a woman, crying bitterly. It was then that he noticed the pile of boards that lay criss-crossed beside the house.

He rushed forward to cut down the cow with his knife, but it was too late. She fell down dead. Then he turned to the woman.

"How could such a thing happen? How did a cow ever get up there in the first place?" he asked in bewilderment.

"Oh, it was like this. See that stand of grass that grows so rich and green on my sod roof?"

He nodded. It was indeed rich and green.

"I thought that grass would be good for my cow, so I put up the boards, and I pulled and I pulled my cow until I got her to climb the boards. Then I tied her to the chimney, but she got too near the edge and fell off, and there she hung." She looked at him wildly through her tears.

"Lady," he said. "Anyone could see that your roof is too steep for a cow, and even if it wasn't, a roof is no place for a cow. It is a shame, but there is only one thing for you to do and that is to get yourself another cow."

Then he shook his head in disgust and passed on down the road. "Surely," he said to himself, "that one is even more stupid than my Bergit. Even she would have better sense than that."

The next noon, his eye caught an occasional flash of sunlight glinting on metal. It was a bright flash and quite dazzling. It interested him. It came from a cluster of farm buildings, and as he drew closer he was surprised to see a woman run out of the house, holding a large flat silver pan. She held it in the sunlight for a moment, and then dashed back into the house. Almost immediately she reappeared with the pan only to dash inside again. Torger watched this strange performance from a distance for a time, but then his curiosity overcame him. He went forward to ask her what she was doing.

She was a neat little person in a big clean apron. "Oh," she said, "my house is so dark inside, I can hardly see anything. I have only the door, you see, and that one little dark window under the eaves, so when the sun shines brightly, I run outside with an empty silver pan. I hold it until it is full of sunshine, and then I run back in with it as fast as I can to empty it, but it doesn't seem to help. It is still dark inside, and I can never carry enough in."

Torger was aghast. "Woman," he asked, "do you have an ax and a saw?"

"Yes, of course," she answered.

"Bring them to me."

He went to the sunlit side of her house, and in one day had cut in a huge window and set in the glass. She had watched the whole procedure with apprehension in the beginning, but when the sunlight poured into her room, her face glowed. "You are a smart man," she said admiringly, "and I am a rich widow, but I could figure no way to fix my house, and yet I like to live here. Now I wish to pay you very well, for you have given me contentment." And she did. The last he saw of her, she was waving and smiling beside the pan which lay forgotten in the grass.

He shook his head in disbelief. "There is the second woman more stupid than my Bergit," he said in wonder as he trudged on.

The next day he came upon a magnificent farm nestled in the trees which skirted a lush meadow. He looked admiringly about as he approached to ask directions for the quickest route to the next town. A sad-faced woman in black opened the door at his knock. He knew by her dress that she was in mourning and had experienced a recent bereavement, but she gave him directions pleasantly, and then asked him quietly, "And from where do you come then?"

"Romerike," he mumbled, hoping she didn't have relatives there.

"Himmerike!" she exclaimed in great excitement. "If you just came from there, then you must know my Edvard. His horse fell on him just last month, and now he is up there with the angels. Tell me, how is my Edvard?" Her eyes were full of tears as she gazed imploringly into his face.

Torger looked into her brimming eyes and made up his mind. If this foolish woman thought that he had just come down from heaven and so knew her Edvard, he wasn't going to disappoint her.

"Yes. Yes, I did see him. He is just fine—fine."

The woman's eyes glittered with tears of joy. "Oh, that is such good news! I am so glad! Is he happy then?"

"Quite happy," Torger assured her.

"Does he need anything? I would love to send anything he needs back with you."

"Well," he said hesitantly, "he could use some fine blankets, a few choice hams, a side of beef—"

"Oh," she cried ecstatically. "I'll get the things I know he enjoyed. I know best what my dear man liked. You must take a buggy and a horse, too, for you can never carry all the treats that my dear Edvard must have."

Torger shrugged, and after the lady had loaded down the new buggy with a fortune in good things, he picked up the reins, but the lady stopped him.

"Just one thing more," she begged. "Can you wait until I can tuck in a bag of gold? I have so much that I can never use it all, and Edvard can go and buy the little treats that he loved so dearly." Then she hurried back into her house.

Torger surveyed all the treasures in the shiny new buggy, and then he studied the fine lines on the spirited black mare. "This one is more stupid than my Bergit," he muttered, "and this one makes the third." So when the widow had stuffed the pouch of gold into the carriage, Torger turned the buggy about and started home—a richer and wiser man.

"I will never be impatient with my little Bergit again," he promised himself.

Why, even she would know the difference between Romerike and heaven! And one thing is for sure—she would never think of me as coming from heaven. I was a lucky man and I didn't know it."

Then he grinned shame-facedly to himself when he thought of his temper with Bergit, and the little mare trotted briskly along. After all, a man could forgive a woman's foolishness once in awhile—and it was especially easy if she had a sweet smile and dimples and shining golden hair. And Bergit did.

3. IMAGINATION

The old white-haired man glared about the kitchen table. "Three sons I have who are a credit to me—workers and dependable, and then there is you—the fourth!" He exploded in anger and confusion at his youngest son. "Why can't you work beside the others? What is it with you that makes a wanderer—a nomad out of you? Don't you want to make an honest living?"

"Yes, but I want to sell things to people who need them. Isn't that—"

But he got no further. "Needles, thimbles, pins, knitting supplies? Every woman worth her salt in Norway has her own supply already. Norwegian women are thrifty. They won't buy something they don't need, and you will starve. That's the direction you are heading." The old man's eyes were flashing as he spoke.

"Why, then I'll have to starve, I suppose," the young man smiled agreeably, his white teeth gleaming. "Or I might try a little imagination."

"Imagination! A fool's business—how can that buy food?" the old man shouted.

"I won't know until I try, Father. Now I must be off. I am sure I will be all right, so don't worry."

"You'll come home when you are starving," the old man muttered gloomily, but his wife silently packed a package of bread and cheese into the pocket of her son's coat, and then she squeezed his arm.

"Take care, Leif," she muttered softly as he closed the door. At least she is on my side, Leif thought as he started out with his pack on his back.

"Breta, we have spoiled him. He is not like the others. What is it with him and this thing called imagination?" the old man asked bitterly.

"I don't know, Knute. But he is young and he will learn. It isn't always wrong to be different," she said, hoping to comfort him. Then she set before him a steaming cup of coffee. "Drink this, and don't grieve so," she urged as she watched with worry the slumped figure of the old man. "Sometimes a child can surprise you. Perhaps it will be so with Leif."

"Let us hope so," the old man sighed.

But Leif loved the warm sun on his back and the freedom to be traveling down the road. He laughed at a red bird that hopped from reed to reed in the ditch. It was an enchanting summer morning with the dew on the grass and the towering mountains gleaming in the sun. He squeezed his mother's package and remembered her good cheeses which made his mouth water, so after a little, he sat down by a trickling water-fall and ate all his mother's good food. It made him feel full and happy. Now he was ready to take over the world as a salesman.

As he came up to his first farmhouse, he hunched his knapsack full of trinkets high on his shoulders, and hurried forward confidently. He found the housewife hanging her clothes in the sun to dry. He had hardly begun his sales speech when she chased him angrily from her yard.

"I have knitting needles—too many of them! And I have too many children to knit for, too," she scolded, as he backed away. "Now go away and stop bothering me."

"My, such a wretched woman," he muttered as he started for the next farm. But here he had no better luck. She, too, ushered him out, annoyed at being bothered on such a busy day as wash day.

"Well," he said aloud, "perhaps father was right. They won't buy needles. But I still haven't tried my imagination. What is it that a truly good housewife likes most?" He thought of his mother. She liked to be praised—he remembered how her cheeks would grow pink and her eyes would sparkle when he would tell her what a good cook she was. It had always gotten him the biggest slice of her fresh Jul bread—a trick that he had discovered early. And yet, he knew there were times when she was hard-pressed to serve them her wonderful food. How his mother enjoyed an economical recipe as every frugal housewife should! He had it! He would give away a recipe that no woman could resist, and then they wouldn't chase him out!

He hurried forward confidently; his quick mind told him that a prosperous-looking farmhouse would be his best bet, for a woman in such a house would already know how necessary it was to be economical. This one would appreciate him! As he expected, though, the woman frowned when she saw his knapsack. "Go away," she said crossly before he had time to boom out a greeting. "I am not interested in buying anything today."

"Well, that's good," he answered smiling, "because I am not selling anything at the moment. I am giving something away."

The woman looked suspicious, but then curiosity got the best of her. She opened the door just a trifle wider. "Yes?" she said hesitantly. "Are you sure it is something free?"

"Yes," he said, his teeth flashing in a boyish smile. "You know that my mother is the best cook in the whole world and the most economical. She knows how to make a little go a long way, but then she had to—she had four of us boys to raise, and we liked to eat."

The woman nodded. "Yes, I know. I raised five, but what has that got to do with what you are giving away free? You better not be wasting my time."

"I am giving away her recipe for making soup—the best soup in the world, and she made it with just water, salt and a nail."

"Soup from a nail!" the woman exclaimed in disbelief. "But that's impossible. "You can't make soup from a nail."

"Oh, yes, you can," the young man insisted confidently. "And it tastes so good. I would really like to make it for you, and that way you will know her secret. Do you have a large kettle and one bright shiny nail?"

"Everyone in Norway has a nail," she said, opening the door.

"Good! Then I will just teach you her recipe in no time." He opened her door and hurried to stoke up her fire before she changed her mind. She went about getting a big kettle and the nail, and in time at all the nail was dancing about on the bottom of the pot in the boiling water.

Now he picked up his knapsack and opened it on her kitchen table, laying out his wares as attractively as he could. "I don't want you to buy anything," he assured her, "but I know an artistic woman when I see one, and so I think you will enjoy looking over these beautiful silver thimbles. They are a treasure, don't you agree? And it does take a little time for soup to cook, you know." She drew near and examined the thimbles. They were new and shiny.

He strode to the pot and studied the dancing nail thoughtfully for a moment, and then he turned to her. "You wouldn't have just a few good chucks of fresh meat to toss in here, would you? Sometimes my mother did that, and my brothers and I liked it better that way."

"Oh, I have some in the meat house. We just butchered."

"In that case, let's add a bone or two. It won't hurt anything," he said.

She was back shortly with two large bones and a good supply of fine meat chunks which he quickly dropped in. Then he went back to his thimbles while the pot bubbled merrily and an enticing aroma began to fill the room. As he was showing her his scissors, he kept his eye on the pot and the fire blazing.

Just after he brought out the new large-eyed darning needles, he went back to the kettle to taste his soup. He smacked his lips appreciatively, and then thought for a moment.

"It is coming right along. It is very good. Yet, is it possible that you might have a few carrots and a large rutabaga or two to drop in? My mother used to say that vegetables were healthy, and that's why all of us boys grew so big."

"Yes, in my root cellar, I have. Shall I get them?"

"Let me go down there," he insisted, and he came up with some big onions and four large potatoes. "We might as well make this a good healthy soup," he grinned.

In no time he had them ready for the pot. Then he quickly returned to his wares. By now she had set aside a few items that she couldn't resist, but forty minutes later when the vegetables were almost cooked, the little pile had grown, and now he returned to the soup kettle and studied it seriously.

"I have made a bad mistake," he said. "We should have had a cover on this kettle. I don't know what is the matter with me. My mother wouldn't have thought of making soup without a tight cover. But it is not too late, perhaps. Would you have one that fits this pot?"

"Of course," and she hurried to get it.

He fitted it carefully on the pot, and looked at it thoughtfully for a moment. He was getting very hungry—they could eat the soup now or—then he made up his mind. A few minutes more, and he wouldn't starve.

"That's a very good cover," he said.

"Yes, very," she agreed, turning a crochet hook over in her hand.

"Since we have this fine cover, why don't we quickly stir up some dumplings and drop them in here—they'll turn out so light and fluffy with a fine cover like that. I'll bet you make the best dumplings in the world—next to my mother," he said boyishly.

"Well, it's been said so—if I do say so myself" she said, dimpling as she got out her bowl.

He carefully dropped the big spoonfuls into the pot and went back to replacing his wares into his knapsack slowly. He would have a much lighter pack he knew.

Twenty minutes later, he opened the large kettle—the dumpling stood up in crowns of white majestic fluffiness. He looked astonished. "Why, those dumplings look better than my own mother's. I wonder if they really are?"

"Well, you must taste them and see," she said confidently. "I would be so disappointed if you didn't. You see, I really can make dumplings. That's what everybody says."

"Then I will have to try them. I wouldn't want to miss a treat like that. Here, let me dish up the soup." He carefully fished out the nail, and then he dished out enormous bowls of the rich steaming soup each capped with fleecy mounds of her white dumplings.

"Better than my mother's!" he exploded, and then he winked at her. "But don't you ever tell her I said that if you happen to meet her!"

The woman blushed with pleasure. "I will never tell," she said, "but I was so sure that you would like my dumplings."

"And the soup?" he asked.

"Delicious," she ageed.

Soon he was at the door bidding her goodby. His pack was ever so much lighter, and his pockets jingled merrily with coins.

"I don't know how I can ever thank you, young man," she called after him. "Just think—soup on a nail."

"Yes, remarkable, isn't it? And so economical, too, but then it wouldn't have tasted half so good without those wonderful dumplings!" Then he waved to her, and grinned to himself for she was smiling proudly as he strode off.

A little later, he remembered his father's worried face. "Poor father," he said. "He would have had a far merrier life if he had had just a little imagination."

DEAR SPRING SUN

Regine Normann

Translated by Torild Homstad

The sun had returned at last!

One after another the mountain tops caught fire. The snow lay fast on the mountain sides and glistened golden-red against the blue winter sky.—But far below the shimmering light lay deep shadows that varied in color from deep blue on the hillsides to almost black out on the fjord. The shadows clung to the land over which they had ruled so long. They were not about to depart willingly, and filled every hollow, clinging to every rock and curling up tightly around the houses, as if afraid of the menacing power of the sun.

The spring sun had also reached the mountain over Krabvaag.

For two days it lay there before descending farther and farther down the hillsides. First it touched the birch thicket which reached up out of the snow. Then it gathered itself together, casting a fiery glow against the steep mountain walls over the crevices where the darkness pressed inward, and spread itself brightly, glittering, ever-changing, over the white tree-less hillsides.

But the sun wouldn't reach all the way down to Krabvaag for the first time until tomorrow. The people there bustled about getting everything ready to receive it. Lefse was buttered and fattigmann and goro cookies stood on the kitchen counters. Outside in the peat shed juniper branches were cut to spread over whitely-scoured floors. The house had to be festive when the first rays of spring sun entered.

Up at Iversen's house sat his old mother. Fire crackled in the stove and cast fingers of light out into the room, where they were swallowed by the daylight. Only over in the corner by the bed did it spill over the flowered bedspread and flicker up the wall to the picture of Christ with the red drops of blood falling from his crown of thorns. The old woman sat at the table. Her feeble, tear-filled eyes strained toward the mountain, while her fingers stroked alternately over a worn almanac and an open hymn book. A seven year old girl stood beside her and looked curiously at the red marks her grandmother had made in the almanac.

"How far has the sun come now?" asked the grandmother.

"It's come as far as Rypaasen."

She sighed. In another quarter hour it would be at Neverbakken.—"Here, take the book and run over to Neverbakken. When you get there, stand still with your back to the sun, without looking at it first. Hold the book so the sun will shine on the pages when you open it. But just as you open the book, say 'Dear Spring Sun, choose a hymn for grandmother!'—Do this three times, but remember to put a bookmark in each time so I can find the hymn again."

Neverbakken lay barren in the blue-gray shadows. Here and there a juniper stuck out of the snow, and a few clumps of birch stood with finely powdered branches. A grouse nibbled at a juniper berry, looked around with sharp black eyes, nibbled at another, and continued on. A weasel peered out from behind a rock. The grouse saw it and cackled softly in warning; another grouse appeared out of the birch clumps after the first.

Up over the hillside the child came. She had to cross her skis to keep from falling. In her hand she held her grandmother's hymn book with the silver clasps.

But now the sun had reached the hillside too, and showered her with golden light.—"Sunshine!" the child shouted, and held out her arms to the sun, but quickly remembered her grandmother's warning and turned her back. With trembling fingers she unfastened the clasps and held the book up to the sun:

"Dear Spring Sun, choose a hymn for grandmother!"—As soon as the bookmarks were in place she turned around, and with a last glance at the sun, started for home.

In her room the old woman waited with fluttering heart. Could the child do it? Would she soon know if she were destined to die this year?—Tomorrow the first rays of the spring sun would reach her own room, but she couldn't wait even that long. Her arthritis had been bad the last couple of nights; there was sure to be a change in the weather, and then it could be days or even weeks before the skies cleared again.

And oh, how she had longed to see the sun this year. She had gone through the almanac hundreds of times, studying all the old weather signs and forecasts.—She had marked the days with red crosses. Yes, the Lord knew best, but fear touched her as she set them there to keep track of the days that were left.—And now she would know. Oh, Lord, what if death were close at hand! She was old and tired, but life was precious all the same.

The sun didn't lie. If it touched a funeral hymn, it warned of impending death. It happened the time she lost two of her sons fishing in Lofoten. The hymnal had fallen open to the funeral hymns, and so when the message came, she was, in a way, prepared.

The old, trembling hands folded tightly in her lap, and the lined face under the white, freshly ironed cap closed around a painful memory.

The door was flung open and the child burst into the room, book in hand.

Grandmother took off her glasses, polished them painstakingly, and slowly put them on again; then she took the book, looked once more at the mountain where the glow of the sun was little by little being extinguished, and opened it.

There was the first bookmark. She removed it carefully and read:

Go now and dig my grave,
I am weary and fain would rest.

Solemnly she read the hymn through to the end. Not the least tremor in her voice or trace in the old lined face revealed what she felt. The child stood at her side and felt as if she were in church.

The next marked passage was opened: "With sorrow and wailing observed —," When she reached the second verse—"We shroud the corpse with tears, and lay it silently on the bier" Her voice trembled with suppressed tears, but she forced them back, and continued to read.

Finally she came to the last marker. Her hands shook as she hesitantly smoothed it out. The child moved a step closer. Her lips trembled and she surveyed her grandmother shyly.

The old woman read:

Here I lie, cold and stiff,
wrapped in a shroud, without life.
My cheeks are pale, my—.

Her voice broke. Tear after tear rolled down her wrinkled cheeks and fell on the book. The child threw herself sobbing on to her grandmother's lap. "Grandmother, you won't die! Listen to me—I looked at the sun first!"

A joyous smile lit up the old woman's face. "Praise God, dear child, then of course it doesn't count.—We can do it again tomorrow."

III. HERITAGE: IMAGES AND REFLECTIONS IN A BLUE SKY

THE FOLLOWING PIECES reveal the various ways in which a number of Midwestern writers perceive their own Norwegian heritage experienced through various events and occasions— often remembered from childhood or at least some earlier and perhaps more impressionable time in the lives of the writers. The degree to which various aspects of "Norwegian-ness" come through the stories varies, but a number of concerns and "things that matter" appear in them—dealing with the supposed "coldness" of Norwegian-Americans, the continuing hardships of rural life, some confusion and/or frustration with the Americanizing process and what seems to be an inevitable confrontation with various patriarchies. Since most Norwegians were Lutherans of some synodical affiliation, the church and its proclivity for dissent is another topic. "The church," an uncle once said to me, "is just there. You can love it or hate it, but you can't quite get the steeple out of your eye."

AFTERNOON SLEEP

Robert Bly

I

I was descending from the mountains of sleep.
Asleep I had gazed east over a sunny field,
And sat on the running board of an old Model A.
I awoke happy, for I had dreamt of my wife,
And the loneliness hiding in grass and weeds
That lies near a man over thirty, and suddenly enters.

II

When Joe Sjolie grew tired, he sold his farm,
Even his bachelor rocker, and did not come back.
He left his dog behind in the cob shed.
The dog refused to take food from strangers.

III

I drove out to the farm when I awoke;
Alone on a hill, sheltered by trees.
The matted grass lay around the house.
When I climbed the porch, the door was open.
Inside were old abandoned books,
And instructions to Norwegian immigrants.

HARDANGER FIDDLE ON A
BLUE PRAIRIE WIND

John Solensten

I have always believed that memory has its own logic. My own Norwegian-American heritage is a part of me, not in a system of belief but rather in a number of sporadic recollections which often surprise and sometimes startle me. There is no history, no story as such, and certainly no clear chronology. Remembering is knowing in the timeless present of who we are and what we recall. The connection between remembering and knowing is often so deep it evades us in unself-consciousness. And I would not want to do violence to those loops and circles of recollection. As Meridel Le Sueur learned from Zona, her Indian friend, violence is linear; love spherical and indirect. And, of course, the truth—and there seldom is *one* truth—is discovered somewhere near the center and comes from many voices.

The church—half a block away from my home in a little southern Minnesota town. It is wooden, stern-eyed in its black-framed windows, white as the blaze of sabbath snow under the blue eye of heaven. Half a block away, no excuse for missing church. Inescapable. Forever in your recollection. In Norwegian above the altar the words of reckoning: "This Jesus who was received up into heaven shall come again in the same manner." The pastor—a black Norwegian —swart as an Italian (Was it gypsies in Norway? And when?), Lincolnesque, rising up and down on his toes as he brings the gospel. And the choir—black robed, facing us and rising to sing. "Children of the Heavenly Father." A girl in the choir—face round and bright, cheekbones full and high, making her eyes smile. Love. And she looks back. Oh, love—and beauty. There, gentle in her bones, is Mary J—a cripple, the town switchboard operator, a husk of humanity —but radiant with joy and tall in her singing. She has a voice flawless and clear as her eyes. Oh, the wonder of all the people.

But there is a grimness too—funerals, especially. The departed lying there under a bower of flowers. The old people huddled there on the hard, yellow oak pews. The big old waxed Packard death buggy outside at the curb. The earth, the flesh do not abide the Word says. Yet smell the coffee fumes—breathing up out of the great furnace grill this side of the casket. And with the fumes the rank, sweet smell of cakes intermingled with the odors of sandwiches and cold meat and hot dishes opulent with cheese and cream. In the basement there are women hefting giant blue-gray porcelain coffee pots up on the blue flames rising up out of black grates. Mrs. Dahl has a face like a troll. The earth abides—and the women of the Aide abide. Though men and women come and go, the sermons dissolve in the windy reaches of memory, coffee and cake and sandwiches abide forever. And the women make it so. Men jerk and fight and pass, but in the bowels of the church physical life is celebrated with great love and even—yes— *Livsglaed.* The social Host is lunch served by women.

But a voice intrudes here. Are you making fun of it all? Don't the relatives need to get together and talk? Don't folks come a long way and maybe miss lunch? Miss lunch? No Norwegian ever misses lunch. Though fast falls the eventide there shall be lunch.

Yes, but remember grandfather, a father's voice says. My father drove the buggy for him to the sod house. It had not been a good week for grandfather. He, the pastor, had to confront Anderson, the self-appointed preacher who was going to preach funeral sermons too. He was a frail man—grandfather was—but he stepped up to Anderson and said some things quietly and stood there—his eyes like blue spear points. "You are a good man. You go home and tend your family," he said. But Anderson would not go home. He walked around and around in a circle of terrible anger in the grass muttering, "The priesthood of believers, isn't it? Isn't it?" And he never came to your grandfather's church again.

But that November day on the prairie. Cold and clear. The open grave yawning there on the little slope behind the house, a cow tethered nearby, its bell clanking softly. Inside the sod house the body at one end and a huge table freighted with food—many roasts—on the other. No embalming? No. Who could pay? And the air was cold.

And your grandfather. He said to take the body outside. But it's cold they said. No matter to him he said nodding at the corpse lying there so cold and still. Outside? They were angry at first until he preached and then they listened. What did he say? I don't remember. I only remember his face my father said. My father said he only watched his face. His face was the Word. Oh, yes and he sang, "Behold a Host Arrayed in White." Stomachs growled. Food, Gospel, time, mortality—and there, somewhere in the west where the ship of the sun goes down are the blue regions of God. His favorite season must be winter. Long months of cold witness to it.

Yet summers. Play Annie-Hi-Over the church with a ball that clatters on the shingles bulged with green moss. Clatter the mewing pigeons from the bell loft. White and blue and whippling their wings, they chill the heart, circle and return. Play Annie-Hi-Over until you are tired to death. Pretend you don't hear your mother (poor, haggard soul smelling of cooking and soap—clean even in her kitchen sweat) calling for you. Until the first stars appear—high over. What has the star to say to you?

Mother, I was not kind. I bring you this from school—a card—cut from colored paper with a stiff, clumsy boy hand and glued forever from the glue pot.

"Mother, I love you. You are my Valentine. You're son."

Responsiblity. The children of the Sunday School will knit an afghan for the children of a Foreign Land. Italian children or was it Latvian? Each is to knit one square. But boys don't do such things, my father says. But the freezing children, says Miss Sorenson, showing us how the freezing children shiver. Miss Sorenson, I dropped your knitting needles down the grates of our furnace. They are melted, my father says. On the Sabbath morning of Responsibility Miss Sorenson holds up the afghan to show it to the Sunday School class. Sit there the learn Responsibility, if that is the right word. One square is missing. It is yours. Miss Sorenson's sad face peers through it. Then you shiver. Somewhere another child feels the cold pierce that opening as he lies in the mud of Salerno or some such place. Cold. Greenland's Icy Mountains.

Girls. The Luther League hayride. Lovely and holy license to press and hold and touch—to quickly taste a mouth and let one wet your ear with the wondrous moisture of new juices! Beautiful girls. Sloe-eyed—hints of Lapp blood—sturdy —generous in mouth—lovely and full for winter. Girls titter. Wiggle. In the hay, the reaches and bolsters of the wagon creaking—a redolence of virile horse urine and deep pastures—promises of soft nights center-to-center *after* you marry.

And, once, Sonja Henie at the movies. Your father sitting with you in the semi-dark. In the flashing shadows his face shows he loves her too. On the ice her smiles charm with midnight sun. And then, later, she is in the wooden coziness of a Norwegian bedroom preparing for bed. A young man there waiting for her as she gets ready for BED. Summer night in all the wide winter. Woman is sun warm in darkness. Your father loves her. But your mother. Ah, but she knows. Laughs. Oh, you men, you darn men! she says, making the popcorn later, shaking the black skillet on top of the cast iron stove.

Coming out of the theatre you see the first new Hudson car to come out after the war. It sits under the veils of snow flying over the theatre and the town. At the center of its grill is a blood red medallion. It has no back seat because there are not yet enough parts. But your heart beats with the chrome and lacquer wonder of the thing—come magically out of austere nights of war. The lights are coming on all over the world.

Some of them—the Norwegians—admired the Nazis. Schmeling will win. Yes. Lindbergh says the Germans bring in a new era for the air frontier. Yes. And his father a Socialist—a Swede though. Still. Yet the young Norwegian poet died fighting the German paratroopers—and a distant cousin was cut in half by their machine guns as he skied down at the German convoy. And they imprisoned pastors and took some of the women. And these were men given refuge in Norwegian homes in World War I. Norway defeated in a few days. Yes, We Love This Land Of Ours.

Hamsun. Did you see it in the paper? A traitor, a fascist, or perhaps merely a little crazy. His name in a quaint signature in the guest book at the Flandreau Hotel in Madelia. Worked in the lumber yard there. An aristocrat. Not much of a worker sitting up on the wagon seat there dressed in a Prince Albert suit. They fired him. Claim he connived with the *other* lumber yard and helped them make low bids on barn building. Not like Rolvaag. Back and forth from Norway. Bookish. What did he want here? Nobel prize, hell! He's a damn quisling and should've been shot, the people at the lumber yard said. Visited once, he did. Knew T. S. Eliot, other voices said. Who? Was in on the founding of that Unitarian Church—with that Jansen from Minneapolis. No? Really? The hell you say! Ya, you bet! One of those.

The minister—the Unitarian one—the troubled one. They wouldn't put up with him at St. Olaf. You heard about him—him with the red hair and beard? There was *two* of him, some say. Well, one or both of him sat down in the well in the yard of the church on the hill that 125 stubborn Norwegian Lutherans built out of sheer cussedness. The whole lot of them could not agree on where to build the Lutheran church. So, this Unitarian came down from the cities and converted them. A Unitarian has no creed. No wonder their pastor was confused. Red hair. You could see it looking down in the well if you covered the opening. Up-floating it was and kind of pink. Took a whole bottle of aspirin and jumped in feet first halfway to the center of the earth, to escape heaven maybe.

"We got to use a rope."

But nothing to get hold of—just his neck."

"So?"

"So."

"Up he comes."

"Up he is."

"You sure he's dead?"

"Well," says a farmer—belonged to the other half of the church—the half that stayed Lutheran, "... well, if he wasn't dead down there he got that way coming up."

"You see the rope at his neck? Poor young man!"

"Odin."

"Odin? The town by Butterfield?"

"No. Him—in the old books you can't find no more."

Shadows of myth—the old ones—unspoken by Christian folk. You must be alone and think deep to know it. North. There is a winter beyond the winter survived by hardy souls. It is blue, enternal weather. The wind is a wolf. Ravens appear on the backs of kitchen chairs when the fire goes out. The wind is a wolf. The teeth of the wolf are final and blue. There is no escape. Fires flutter and die. There is no more oil or gas. Wood will not ignite if you can find some. The windows of the church even—are like the eyes of the wolf—a yellow, incandescent mockery. Of course it never happens. Yet they say we are doing things to the land and that we may be punished for those things.

Life is hard. A man is responsible and must provide. Your father is a good provider.

But Mr. Omsrud lost his farm. So they let him stay on it—a renter. Still his eyes look down at his hands. Work is not enough—the sweat of the brow is not enough. It's good land; what happened? No, the farmers don't want to get together like a bunch of Socialists. No, it was Hoover who done it. Hoover is dead. Mr. Omsrud waits in the Lutheran Home. His sons have gone off the land. Couldn't afford to buy it. Mr. Omsud has a secret. In heaven he will kill Hoover—maybe with a pitchfork. God? What the hell does he know? He never had to farm in the Depression.

Aunts come to dinner—everlasting aunts, Ibsen called them. They are often women with iron rods up their spines. They live beyond men and lurk close to the right elbow of God. They do not serve food with the Aide women. They sometimes speak with hoarse voices. Why are they hoarse when they seldom speak? What are they hoarse from? Well, from screaming inside themselves perhaps. Is there anything angrier than a bright woman who has no *good* work to do? Whew!

Aunts come to dinner after church, their backs pew stiff, their eyes looking out through the lace curtains of the dining room to God's wide Sabbath afternoon.

This one is Aunt Cerena. Had three years at St. Olaf—in the choir. Wouldn't teach; wouldn't marry; wouldn't. Father sits at the head of the table but Aunt Cerena presides—smelling of talcum powder and wool and antique chastity. Everyone is polite. Do not offend Aunt Cerena. She is not happy—a bright woman.

The boy has had her for a summer school teacher. There is something about her that compels him to seek her approval—one of her rare, benign smiles.

"Say," he says, a piece of roast pronged on his fork—in transport to his mouth.

A frown. Cut up your meat.

"Say," he says. "Guess what?"

Nothing. But then God has spoken once through the prophets and then . . .

He goes on, the boy. He has everyone's attention. He has been riding around in his uncle's truck. His uncle has a powerful vocabulary through all the gears.

"Well," says the boy, his face glowing with righteous indignation, "This Jimmy Connors traps pigeons and kills and eats them, the dirty Irish son-of-a-bitch!"

Aunt Cerena says nothing. She places her silverware and napkin exactly where she found them. God waits outside—always the gentleman. She gets up in stiff and terrible dignity, thanks the father, moves through the slant of light in the dining room (All faces behind her frozen between horror and laughter) and departs in her black Dodge never to return again until after the whole family, disregarding justification by faith, seeks absolution from her. Oh, God is easy compared to Aunt Cerena.

The father seizes the son and drags him out into the garage. "What's the matter with you?" he growls, biting his own mouth to fight the laughter.

"That's what Uncle Olaf said."

The razor strap. Whap! Whap! Whap!—mostly on air. Whap! Whap!

91

Whap! No tears. The air does not cry.

Those faces. Turn the photos sideways to see what happened before and after the photos. Were the people those faces? Sitting in catechism in the basement of the church—a basement of stones. Your name means sun on stone. Prester. Your grandfather's picture there. The ruffled collar. The gentle mouth. But the eyes. "What are you doing with your life?" they ask. They are cold eyes—severe and unflinching forever in the photo.

Yet there is another photo—really a series of photos—all in the autumnal tones on the thick paper they used in those days. In those days? What year? I don't know.

There is another one—found in father's Chautauqua desk—always locked. Who took such a picture? In American folk art it would be called a memorial picture. Yet this is a graveside. A figure in a black vested suit stands there—a slight figure already bent by life. His face is heavy with the weight of grief as he looks down at a mound of fresh earth. Around him there are infinite distances of deep, tangled prairie grass. At grave's edge the grass seems to lick at the new dirt like dark flames. It is hungry to cover all. I am the grass, the Swede poet says, and I will work.

There is a love story there. Father knows as grandfather did what it is. Find another photo. A young woman's face—19 or so—a bit childlike in its open-eyed directness and small mouth. Listen to the words before it and after it. Matea—sweet-voiced in the choir, love daughter of the congregation. Beloved in the life of the preacher as Ann Rutledge was in the life of Lincoln—the first and perhaps only love. Soon—within the year—she gives birth to a son, your father. The frame house is cold; grandfather out on call. A blizzard rages against the house. To keep warm Matea walks, walks, walks—shielding the child. Fine snow buzzes through the cracks in the walls. And then a certain cough and fever. The horses bring grandfather home through the fury of the snow. He rushes inside and sees the flush on the face. She is even more beautiful then. But pneumonia is not beautiful nor merciful. Pant like a bird and then die:

MATEA

Fodt	6 June 1865
Tod	20 January 1884

The child lives; the preacher marries a tall, strong woman with desperate eyes. She spoiled your father, the aunts said to the boy.

"We should never have left our homeland. Then she would not be dead and this other good woman would not have to live with the photos in the unopened drawer."

"We should fear, love and trust in God above all things ..."

There were books in the drawers—many in Norwegian—but we were not encouraged to learn Norwegian. The Yankees know. They have no barbaric customs like a ludefisk supper. But my mother plays Grieg and my uncle reads

Wergeland the poet whose heart leaps to the window of light. Yes, but New England—the iron dark of it—is already old with the books of America. If there is an American culture it is there. We are Americans now. The McGuffey reader says so and the Chautauqua and the American language and the n.en on the walls of the schoolrooms. Your father's heroes are Bernard Mcfadden, the physical culturist and businessmen like the Cargills and Daytons—Yankee names.

You are sometime embarrassed by "Ya" and Norskie jokes and the thickness of accents. Only the piano teachers or the preacher or the preacher's wife know Grieg. What music shall we have then?

The distant music of the Hardanger fiddle. Sweet and sad, it honks like a goose high on a tight wind. Uncle Edwin plays it, imaginary leaves in his hair. His wife, bent by arthritis into a cruel pretzel of a body, has put candles on the table in a candelabrum from the Old Country—a brass one turned on a hand lathe lovingly. The heron dances far off on Lake Linden. The heart dances with the fiddled eyes. There were two sets of strings on such a fiddle—one for the primary stroke of the bow; one for resonance. We who live in a new time hear only the resonances. And someone lost the fiddle, or perhaps the auctioneer stole it.

So my uncle drank. Good Norwegians do not drink so the bootlegger lives across the street and the front panels of his 1934 Ford contain, behind the mohair, the clinking of bottles. But many are Pietists. Yet why are so many drunk so much? Because they let the bootlegger get by with it. Perhaps it is the Germans in New Ulm. Once, they say, the water was turned off in New Ulm for a whole weekend and no one was thirsty. But my uncle played the Hardanger fiddle and got drunk twice a year and ran all over the country like a tall, red-haired jackrabbit. Slept in haymows. Burst into kitchens for breakfast. Was found sleeping in the rye (and the wry) just beyond the whirling reel of the combine. Couldn't stop him. Wouldn't hear you! Walked off tall. Might as well try to stop the grass from growing.

I hear the prairie wind in the sailor chamber of my heart. I contain the picture of Matea and hold it in unashamed and incestuous love. I am forever stopping by country churches where sweet grandfather sang and the doves cry the paraclete from the cooing steeples. Graves and headstones attend me on Memorial Day. The snow geese sliding on autumn wind over tapestries of green-yellow grass are the great white flock. I hear the dark on a Sunday night and poke at the drapes and search nervously for stars. I am droll and often profane. I am the heir of independent people. I do not understand talkative Irish. I know that my people were undemonstrative, but I have heard many joys in the night where I slept upstairs on farms forever fled now from memory. Yes, America is a good place, but to never hear the Old Music is not so good. And to have nothing wonderful to remember is the worst amnesia—the dull blank of not knowing where we have come from. The prairie wind is blue; the fiddle still plays; no good tune is lost. If we listen.

ANNA CHRISTINA JOHNSON
PLAYS THE SAW

Patricia Zontelli

For her five children, Anna sewed
clothes, baked meat and potatoes
and worked two jobs, two shifts.

For her Presbyterian Church,
Anna vibrated with such ardent
hymns of thanksgiving

the cherries on her felt hat shook, my shy
twice-divorced uncle Lars shrinking down
into the pockets of his Sunday suit. Anna's

entire backyard sprouted garden, not a weed
dared—everything edible glassed into quarts
for her son, Lars, diabetic until at forty-three

he died of it—and of that other,
the heart unmended. For herself,
Anna played the saw

in the cellar amidst the coal smell, coal
furnace, jars of pickles, pears, piccalilli,
chow-chow, melon-rind and rhubarb

under a bare light bulb my grandmother Anna
played the saw, wiggling the tip
of it "just so" to make the eerie

unpredictable Norwegian melody flitter
into air—with such
dancing in her blue eyes

94

the house danced, the garden swayed,
the oriental glass windchimes
on her front porch shivered

beginning its careful, delicate applause.

OLE LARSEN, 1806-1871

Doug Johnson

I

In a dream,
starry night,
you step from the trees: the good eye
clear with a cold light blue,
pious Moravian,
bearded with the frost of a hundred seasons,
feet wrapped
in the birch bark and moss of the other world.

II

In winter,
seventy miles on foot
with a load of frozen fish ...

Did you tell stories to your pony, or yourself,
on the long treks over the bay?

Tales of Draugs
and the Lapps with their mystical reindeer.

III

Today I stumbled among roots
of your pine and cedar.
Lay down in a soft bed of needles.
Forgot the oppression
of suburbs.

Cedars grope along limestone,
seeking the least hint of nourishment.
They lean out over jagged cliffs:

the grieving wives
of lost sailors.

But the sorrow in the soul of the trees
is not a human sorrow.

IV

Typical American,
you cleared the island of its timber
in just three years.
Disassembled your log house.
Invaded the mainland.

Now the trees are back.
Tourists from Chicago
moor sleek yachts in the little harbor;
they come to picnic
near the lost bones of Norwegians.

*This was written in the fall of '82 and is about my
great great grandfather, a Norwegian immigrant who was
the first white settler in Door County, Wis. He urged
a group of Norwegian Moravians to settle there, where
they founded the colony of Ephraim.*

SUMMER SALVATION

Solfrid Aslanian

My childhood had no doubt already shaped me into an odd-ball. I had been uprooted from Norway when I was four, from America when I was nine, and then again from Norway when I was twelve. My parents were torn between their love of both countries—between old loyalties and new opportunities. Since I was so young, adaptation had been relatively easy; it was mostly a matter of learning how to dress and talk like the other kids around me. Before the summer of 1957, when I was thirteen, I didn't understand that there were lines to be drawn, that going beyond them meant not adaptation but total surrender.

The summer of 1957 was a long, lazy summer—an endless string of sunny days, unusual for Seattle. I was one of those lucky kids who had no chores or responsibilities beyond making my bed in the mornings and pulling a few weeds from the garden once a week or so. My parents, both of them from large, hard-working families, decided that their own two daughters should have a chance to enjoy their youth. As my mother put it, "When you grow up and have responsibilities, you can never be free to do as you please. Childhood is the only time it is possible to do that." Thus, every day that summer, the question of what I should do was answered the same way: go to the beach with Dianne, Darlene, Kathy, and Joanne.

The beaches were just a short distance from my house. Around 10:00 each morning, we set off down the steep hill, carrying our loads of blankets, towels, snacks, and portable radios. Golden Gardens, a section of the beach area, was a friendly place. We always met other kids we knew and, usually, several more girls would join our little colony on the sand. We lay on the beach for hours—skinny bodies smeared with concoctions of baby oil and iodine—listening to KJR, Seattle's top rock station. We knew the order of the songs on the hit charts and carefully monitored the rise and fall of our favorites. Wistfully, we heard the disc jockeys announce the local bands that would be appearing at the dances for the high school kids. At intervals, we cooled off by wading in the 55 degree water of Puget Sound, keeping our one-piece suits dry until the high tide rolled in over the sun-warmed sand. We knew it was time to head home for supper when the sun approached the tops of the Olympic Mountains, directly across the Sound from where we were.

By August, however, my enjoyment at the beach had become blunted by a vague sense of monotony. I was ready for a change. When Reidun, a girl who lived across the street, invited me to go with her and her friend, Inger, to their church camp, I leaped at the chance. I suspected my inclusion came only because Reidun and Inger had only recently immigrated from Norway and didn't have many American friends yet. Still, I was flattered to be invited by these two older girls and I nurtured pleasant memories of my own church camp experience the summer before. The Lutheran church was something I was comfortable with; it had been a constant in my life, in America and in Norway, and I had never given it much thought. Lutherland, my own church camp, served kids from all over the Seattle-Tacoma area and had been filled that year when Joanne and I tried to sign up.

I packed my suitcase carefully, making sure I had swimming suits and shorts. At Lutherland, we played softball or volleyball in the afternoons. Afterwards, we'd go swimming. There was a raft to swim out to and boats to go rowing in. I guessed I'd need a sweatshirt and a windbreaker if it got cold at night, when we sat around the campfire, singing and roasting marshmallows. I wondered whether there'd be a place to buy pop and candy at the new camp. That had been the most fun last year—lying in our bunks, whispering and eating candy after lights out. One night, we even sneaked out of our cabin and ran around on the trails in the woods between the cabins. We were going to play a prank on the boys' cabin, but our counselor rounded us up before we got that far. She wasn't even mad. Yes, Lutherland had been a good place. I even liked the morning Bible classes. They were led by a cute young pre-seminarian from Augsburg College.

On Sunday afternoon, when Reidun's father pulled up in front of our house and I got into the car, I noticed that Reidun and Inger were wearing skirts and white blouses. I had changed into my pedal pushers after I came home from church. Maybe Reidun and Inger would change at camp.

"The drive is not so far, I think," said Reidun, turning around to face me from the front seat. "Perhaps one half hour."

"Ja, the school it is just beyond—what do you say?—city limit," said Reidun's father.

"School?" I said, surprised.

"Ja. Gethsemane is a school, too. I go there next year," said Inger, "when I can drive a car myself."

Well, I thought, maybe it's like a college campus—like Pacific Lutheran, where my sister was a student. A campus was big enough to have a lake on it.

After that, the small talk continued in Norwegian. It wasn't necessary to make the effort to speak English since all of us spoke Norwegian, even though different dialects. Reidun's English was better than Inger's and she already looked pretty American. Her brown hair was cut short and curled around her rather plain face. Inger had long, blond hair, not unlike my own. She would have been almost pretty, I thought, if she lost a little weight and if her teeth didn't stick out so far. Neither Reidun nor Inger wore any lipstick, even though they were sixteen. I had started using lipstick the previous year, in seventh grade. All my friends wore lipstick.

"Here we are," said Mr. Eidseth as he drove us through the front gates. I saw big tan-colored buildings on both sides of the drive, concrete sidewalks practically meeting the brick walls. Old people walked with canes or were being pushed in their wheelchairs. Sprinklers were whirring over the rectangles of close-clipped lawn on either side of the drive.

"Is this where the camp is?" I burst out.

"This is the old people's home. The school is just over there." Reidun pointed to a couple of buildings farther down the road. They looked exactly like the first ones—hardly any trees around: a few lonely fir trees and a clump of young maples.

The uneasiness which crept over me with the sight of the tan block buildings did not ease when we arranged our sleeping bags on the wire cots in the dormitory room. It was hospital clean, its tiled floor gleaming and smelling of Pine-Sol. There were four beds and a metal chair. A tiny mirror hung by itself next to the door which opened to the long hallway. I thought about the cozy log cabins at Lutherland, the smell of real fir and pine which blew in the open windows from the woods of the lake. I felt a big lump in my throat.

My hopes for a good time collapsed altogether when we went to the dining hall for dinner and I saw the week's schedule: morning and afternoon Bible classes followed by evening meetings; brief mealtime recesses—maybe a few mintues to punch the tetherball on the pole outside the cafeteria. It would be a long week. I sighed. At least I had brought my radio. I had seen some cute boys at dinner, but they were too old for me. Last year, Ron, a cute boy from Tacoma, had sent me a present after I came home from camp. It was a "book"—when you opened it up, it had five rolls of Life-Savers on each side. Ron and I wrote letters back and forth for a while, until we ran out of things to say. I could tell I wouldn't meet a new boyfriend at Gethsemane.

I tagged along with Reidun and Inger to Bible classes the next day. The scriptures were familiar enough, but I found the classes long and boring. Still, the teachers were kindly and these older kids seemed to take the lessons seriously, so I tried very hard to be good also and think religious thoughts.

The evening meeting in the great hall began with hymn singing: "The Old Rugged Cross" and "Amazing Grace." Then, a middle-aged man with a balding head and intense eyes began to speak. He talked about the Christian way of life and how we couldn't be saved until we accepted Christ as our savior. He invited us to testify about our personal experiences. I had heard ministers and missionaries speak of their own experiences, but I had never been in a gathering where people in the congregation stood to speak. After a brief pause, a boy who was sitting behind us rose and began speaking.

"I want to testify," he began in a low, halting voice, eyes looking down at the floor, long arms hanging awkwardly, hands folded in front of him. "Before I accepted Christ as my personal savior, I was a juvenile delinquent."

I listened intently. I'd never known a juvenile delinquent. He certainly looked like an ordinary boy—crewcut hair, plaid shirt, suntans.

"My parents brought me up in a Christian home. I thought they were too strict. I started sneaking around behind their backs to be with my friends. I got in with the wrong crowd. We'd go out cruising in fast cars with fast girls. To wild parties with wild music, dancing, and drinking." He drew a deep breath. "One night, the police came and raided a party. We were all drunk. They brought us to the police station and called our parents." He hesitated.

"That was the worst experience I've ever had in my life. I'll never forget the heartbroken looks on my mom and dad's faces when they walked into that police station. But it made me see the light. Made me see the path that I was on. I decided to turn my life over to the Lord. I'm praying that my friends will, too."

The boy sat down. The group, about seventy teenagers and a handful of adults, sat quietly, expectantly. A plump girl, about sixteen or seventeen, with fluffy blond hair, stood up. She fidgeted with the buttons on her pink overblouse.

"Before I found Jesus, I was always afraid of being unpopular. My parents didn't seem to care very much about me. They were always so busy working. I really wanted a boyfriend, but I—I had a hard time. Oh, they asked me out all right. But never the same boy twice. I thought it was because I was too square and didn't neck with them. So then, I began to—" She tossed her hair back—"I stopped saying no. But things didn't change—they still didn't call back." Her voice became almost inaudible.

"One day, at school, I was walking behind two boys I had dated and I heard one of them laugh when he said my name. 'She's so easy, she'll do it with anyone,' I heard him say. I was so upset, I turned around and ran out of the school. Home. I wanted to die. So that's what I decided to do."

She trembled and her eyes filled with tears. The room was utterly quiet.

"But I woke up in a hospital room. Now, I'll always have this reminder"— (she held out her wrists)—"but it will help me remember that Jesus is the only savior. All I'll ever need is Him."

Her ugly, scarred wrists made me shudder. Their image kept reappearing before me as I listened to the continuing testimonials. All the kids seemed to have started out as ordinary teenagers. All of them got into trouble because they strayed from Christ. Most of the stories involved getting in with "the wrong crowd." I began to wonder whether I was saved. I hadn't ever made a conscious decision to be a Christian; it was just something that was there, a given, whether I was in Norway or in America. I couldn't think of anything really bad I had done, but I couldn't think of anything particularly good, either. I loved rock 'n roll music and spent hours reading fan magazines rather than the Bible. My sister said I was boy-crazy. Maybe I wasn't saved. I looked over at Reidun and Inger, sitting beside me. They hadn't stood up, but they both had tears running down their faces. Reidun was blowing her nose in a falling-apart kleenex. Maybe they weren't saved either?

The organist began to play "Just as I Am" and the preacher spoke above the soft strains of the music.

"Jesus wants you to come forward to accept the gift of his salvation. To stand up and be counted as one of his children."

It seemed like everyone got up, almost like at Holy Communion at my church. When Reidun and Inger stood up, I hurriedly rose and followed them to the little platform. The organist continued to play. We kneeled down. When I saw the bowed heads, I too, closed my eyes. I became aware of the lyrics of the music: "Just as I am/ And waiting not/ To rid my soul/ Of one dark blot ..." Everyone sang, all around me. Suddenly, I felt a light tap on my shoulder and opened my eyes. It was the gray-haired lady who had conducted the morning Bible class. Her face beamed ecstatically.

"Come, let's go and find your Bible," she whispered. Meekly, I stood up and walked toward the vacant metal chairs and found my familiar black Bible. My parents had given it to me on my eighth birthday, because I had wanted one like my older sister's.

"We must mark this day in your Bible," the woman said.

"Where should I mark it?" I asked, bewildered. She flipped quickly through the thin, crinkly pages to Romans 10:13: "For whosoever shall call upon the name of the Lord shall be saved." Obediently, I wrote "Aug. 13, 1957." I stared at the cramped figures I had squeezed into the narrow right hand margin.

"Now, dear, let's pray," she smiled and kneeled before my metal chair. "Let's thank Him for saving you."

I felt my face flush. I wanted to get up and run away, to be home. But I got on my knees beside her, not hearing what she prayed, distracted by my confusion, focusing upon the strange sheen of her navy blue dress next to the floor.

Finally, the organist stopped playing "Just as I Am" and I saw Reidun and Inger slip into their seats. The woman got up with a "God Bless You" and the minister intoned a closing prayer. I began to breathe easier. At least now I can get away from all this, I thought, as we slowly shuffled out the doors.

Silently, the group walked the little distance from the meeting house to the dormitory. I could hear sniffles among some who were walking behind us. Tomorrow, I thought, things will be normal again and people will talk about ordinary, everyday things.

A little while after I had snuggled into my familiar old sleeping bag and was nearly asleep, I was startled wide awake again. Someone was crying. It came from the room next door. Anguished sobs that sent shivers down my back. It was pitch black, so I could gain no reassurance from being in the next room. Reidun and Inger lay silently—perhaps they were sleeping?—so I said nothing to them. Besides, I didn't know what to say. Maybe they were used to this? I covered my ears with my pillow, trying to drown out the cries. They sounded like those of an injured animal, not quite human, Please God—I prayed earnestly now, but silently—please get me out of this place! Make Saturday come fast.

I heard footsteps and then muffled voices. Finally, it became quiet and I fell asleep, huddled as far down into the bottom of my sleeping bag as I could get.

The next morning, I awoke to the sunshine streaming into the room. Reidun's and Inger's beds were empty. Evidently, they had already gone down the hall to the bathroom. As I opened my suitcase to get my clothes, I saw my beloved portable radio. I turned it on and heard a burst of Chuck Berry's "Sweet Little Sixteen." Boy, I thought, will it be fun to be at Golden Gardens again! I was almost cheerful. But at that moment, Reidun appeared at my side.

"What are you listening to? That's worldly music. Have you forgotten last night?"

I felt like I had been slapped. Inger and some of the other girls were standing in the doorway looking at me with reproachful eyes. Hot with embarrassment but also a prickling resentment, I quickly snapped the knob and thrust the radio into my suitcase. "Oh," I mumbled. Saturday seemed a long time away.

I went through the remaining four days woodenly, attending the Bible classes with utter detachment. It was as if I were encased within a thick glass bubble. I could see enough to go through the appropriate motions, but nothing had anything to do with me. At each evening meeting, more campers continued to go forward. I averted my eyes and gritted my teeth.

Saturday came at last. Mr. Eidseth picked us up. Reidun and Ingar babbled happily about what a great revival it had been. Many had been saved, they told him, and they looked at me. I didn't care what they said now; I was almost home.

When the car stopped by our back gate, I saw my father painting the back porch stairs—my lovely, kind, calm father, doing a normal, everyday kind of thing! Grabbing my suitcase and sleeping bag from the car trunk, barely managing the required thank-you's, I broke into a trot and ran up the walkway to my father. I flung my arms around his neck so hard he almost knocked over the can of brick red paint. "Daddy!"

He seemed pleased but surprised at this unusually warm greeting. Before he could say anything, I bombarded him with questions: "Daddy, do you think it's sinful to listen to rock 'n roll music? To dance? To go to parties? To have fun?"

I saw his brows furrow. He scratched his chin thoughtfully, but he didn't interrupt me.

"Daddy, do you think I'm bad? Do you think I'm saved even if I do like all those things?" I waited breathlessly, desperately, for his answer. Something was happening around the corners of his mouth. He was smiling!

"Bad? Bad?" he repeated. "Of course not, my little one. Some people are a little extreme. They mean well, but they have a funny way of looking at things. Talk to your mother about it. She understands it better than I do. She's at the grocery store, but she'll be back in a few minutes."

But it didn't matter. I was already free again. I ran upstairs to my bedroom. How wonderful to see that wall covered with pictures of Elvis! I turned on the radio. The voices of Buddy Holly and the Crickets filled the room. Then I ran back downstairs to call Dianne. We would go to Golden Gardens the next morning. Dianne told me that the baby oil mixture was even better if we added vinegar. Elvis' record was number one on the charts.

103

PAPA'S GIFT: A RED RIVER VALLEY STORY

Clarice Olson Adelmann

I was not prepared for Nature's tricks during my thirteenth summer, although acceptance of constant change lies at the heart of life on the farm. I knew, of course, that a mewling kitten will soon become a scrapping barnyard tom, that tender saplings will after a few years support the weight of children playing Tarzan, that the freshly turned loam of springtime will by late summer cradle a lush stand of grain, and that a wobbly-legged calf was best not named lest the imminent arrival of the cattle truck cause too much pain.

These patterns of growth were all well and good for animals and plants but intolerable when applied to me. I resented the signs of maturation occurring in my body—embarrassing nubbins of breasts which meant hiding under baggy shirts rather than going about bare-topped as I'd often done before on sultry days. Soon, I knew, I faced the lot of women—the monthly curse of belts and flannel pads, of cramps and swelling—a prospect too dismal to contemplate.

I felt wretched and alone, broody and cranky. No longer was it seemly to climb onto Papa's lap, as Carl and Ellen did. Ma's appraising eyes often followed me, causing me to waspishly snap, "What are you looking at?" before scrambling up the ladder, bound for the steamy seclusion of my attic retreat.

I welcomed the fall opening of school, comforted to note that several girls slumped just as I did under their blouses, that they too opted for dungarees rolled up to mid-calf rather than too short, too snug dresses. We could have shared confidences, talking over the disturbing business of growing up, but shyness damned each of us to suffer and worry alone.

As Christmas drew near and with it the impending church program, Ma checked over our clothes. Carl's suit could be lengthened, although the sleeves were a big short; Ellen could wear one of my outgrown frocks; nothing fit me. I felt guilty. The record-setting spring flood in 1948 had shortened the growing season, resulting in a skimpy harvest. Aware of our family's shaky financial straits, Ma fretted. The costly dried apricots, prunes, and raisins for the fruit soup and even the lutefisk had not yet been bought for the Yuletide celebration. Yet, there was no choice but for us to make a trip to town to outfit me properly. Far better to forgo the usual Christmas fare than to risk pity from any critical eyes at Kongsvinger Lutheran.

After the fifteen-mile trip into town along the wind-swept gravel roads of the Valley, we pulled up at the creamery where Papa lifted the heavy cream can unto the loading dock. Ma and I took chairs in the drafty office to wait for the results of the cream test and subsequent payment. An hour later, we were ready to start the trek to the west side.

"Tie your scarf tighter," Ma said, as we neared the bridge that spanned the frozen Red River separating East Grand Forks from Grand Forks.

Although we walked at a brisk clip, our noses dripped and our feet felt numb when we reached the Dakota side of the river. Grateful for the warmth of Herberger's, Ma steered me to the box-like garments in the children's department. Shaking her head in exasperation, she held dresses up to me. Too short. We headed for the women's sizes. Too big. I knew I was a freak.

"Mom, maybe Buttrey's would have something."

"Buttrey's! You know we can't afford that store."

"They have junior sizes in there, Ma—kinda in-between."

She shrugged. "We can look, but I doubt that any place can take care of a colt."

Bristling, I held my tongue. It was in the window—the dress I had spotted as we swept past earlier.

"Isn't it pretty, Ma?"

"The price is pretty, too. Can you imagine—$8.99 for a girl's dress! Think what the old man would say!"

However, I did not yet have a dress, and the Christmas program was just two weeks away. Before we pushed through the revolving door, Ma stuffed her worn mittens deep into the pockets of her coat. "Come then," she said. "I guess they can't charge us for looking."

Ill at ease amid the elegant trappings of the store, we ignored the clerks and headed straight for the dress racks.

"I'll try them on by myself," I told Ma, selecting a size 7 and a size 9.

"Yah, go," she answered, flinging off her coat and tugging at her constricting corset as she sank gratefully into a chair.

The size 7 was perfect, but one must consider future growth. With that in mind, I emerged from the fitting room wearing the larger size. Grudgingly Ma conceded, "It fits you good."

I dared not respond, holding my breath as she fingered the ten-dollar bill from the creamery.

"There'll be hell to pay," predicted Ma as we again crossed the bridge to the east side where Papa waited in the Model-A in his customary parking spot across from the Great Northern depot. But when she slapped the store receipt into the palm of his leather mitten, he said only, "The cream-can will be full again before Christmas."

*   *   *   *   *

The dress was beautiful—of fine red wool, with small darts at the bustline, gold buttons on the bodice, fashionable three-quarter length sleeves, and a waistline defined by a slim belt. Each time my parents went to do chores, I tried it on again, exulting as the full skirt flared out in a scarlet circle as I executed dizzying pirouettes.

After rummaging in the attic through boxes of clothes discarded by older sisters, I found a worn and gray brassiere, the elastic stretched and the straps frayed. I mended and altered the garment, pleased with the new silhouette reflected by the cracked mirror of Ma's dresser. However, my flour-sack petticoat ruined the entire effect. I'd go without and not tell Ma.

There was yet a problem. Anklets didn't look right with the dress; neither did my brown cotton stockings. The box of attic discards held only a few mismatched nylons with so many runs that they were of use for but one purpose—to anchor tomato plants to stakes.

A few days before the Christmas program, I asked Ma as Papa napped in the bedroom off the kitchen, "What will I wear—anklets or brown stockings?"

Pausing a moment before resuming kneading a large mass of bread dough, she said softly, "Take your choice. I know what you're wishing for, but we can't have everything. Be grateful for the dress."

I flushed. "Yah, Ma, I know."

*   *   *   *   *

On the morning of the program, Papa muttered that he was running short of Copenhagen snuff, necessitating a trip to Oslo, nine miles away. Almost three hours later, the Model-A coughed back into the yard. The kitchen door burst open and, with the unmistakable odor of brandy fouling his breath, Papa thrust two slim packages toward Mom. "For you," he said gruffly, "... and for her." Abruptly, he grabbed his chores cap and headed for the barn.

"Have you ever!" Ma marveled, as she opened the packages that revealed nylon stockings. The larger pair meant for her was regulation beige with a simple seam. Mine was not. The dark hose with an embroidered, garish design starting at the heel and running half-way up the calf might have been a fine choice for a streetwalker. But I rejoiced at the gift.

The church that evening held the magic air of festivity that always marked Christmas celebrations in our Norwegian tradition. I wore my snow-pants under my dress and removed them after I was seated in the pews reserved for Sunday School children. Although astonished seatmates stared at my black legs, I sat with head held high, fighting the urge to run my fingers over the foreign silkiness sheathing my thin limbs.

When the time came for our group's medley of Christmas songs and rehearsed "pieces," we lined up at the altar, I in the last row as befitted those tallest and due to be confirmed.

Searching out my parents, I found Ma next to Mrs. Hendrickson in the center section and at last spotted Papa in one of the south pews reserved for men of the congregation. As our eyes met and locked, his face shadowed briefly and suddenly he looked old. It was an illusion, of course, for he quickly straightened his shoulders just as he was wont to do. Then with his blue eyes still fastened on me, he slowly and solemnly inclined his head in the salute he reserved for womankind, not for girl children. My throat tightened; yet my heart sang.

An acknowledgement of the tribute was needed, just as I'd seen ladies in town, visiting aunts, and Ma respond to the greeting. Taking a deep breath, I too nodded ever so imperceptibly, unable to restrain a tremulous smile. Papa, I knew then, had helped me cross an invisible line. And there was no turning back.

DR. HENRY M. SIMMONS

Brenda Ueland

My father came from Norway when he was 17, dug the Washington Avenue sewer and became a lawyer when he was 26. My mother was born in Ohio during the Civil War among Abolitionists rescuing runaway slaves. She went to high school in Minneapolis and although very poor, she had great beauty and style. After high school she taught Sixth Grade and years later, one of her pupils told me: "I was never bright until I was in your mother's class and I have been bright every since." And I understood so well what he meant.

My parents were political idealists, femininsts, democrats. They wanted their children to be light-hearted and athletic, to live outdoors and eat oranges and apples. My mother thought the girls should not be the menials of the boys and so the boys made their own beds and the girls were on the football team in the pasture. She thought that if mothers were what they should be, surrounding their children with every freedom and happiness and cheerful intelligence, we would have the Millennium in one generation. She taught the baby how to hold and smooth the cat. She never cautioned us. We could walk endless miles in the country, swim across the lake, ride bareback. Our adventurousness was never quashed. She would have liked Blake's aphorism: "Prudence is a rich, ugly Old Maid courted by Incapacity."

My father as a small boy herded goats in the mountains in the province of Stavanger where Lutheranism was especially full of vengeful doom. He wrote:

"We really had much fun. Looking far away at the North Sea, what fancies of adventures! I recall only one drawback. That was toward the evening when my brother went out of sight to round up the herd, leaving me alone. Then I would feel the unusual colors in the sky were signals of the Day of Judgment approaching; as in Matthew 24:30. For the moment it made me repentant and pious but I was no sooner home before I was as worldly as ever. It was as though someone in the house could stay the Day of Judgment."

This was the beginning of his impassioned critical search into Religious Orthodoxy to rescue himself and other poor Lutherans from fear of the Devil and Hell. It seemed to him an outrageous concept, ignorant and cruel—eighty-year-old women who had never said "Boo!" to anyone, weeping in terror because they believed somehow that they were going to Hell for their dreadful sins!

In this country he came upon what was called the Higher Criticism of the Bible and Dr. Henry M. Simmons and my parents became Unitarians. Dr. Simmons was the most sincere and compassionate Christian but in his sermons he also talked about Darwin, Erasmus, Plato, about the accuracies of history and archeology. The church was on Mary Place just this side of Dayton's on what is now LaSalle. We drove down there every Sunday with our big horse, Lady Mane and the carriage, a lovely street under arching elms, the only noise the thudding of horses' hooves. It was a plump sturdy church of huge red stone blocks and a fat tower at one end. The sermons were wonderful, the utterance of a true poet and scholar; they might have been written by Coleridge. Our Credo then was: "The Fatherhood of God, the Leadership of Jesus, the Brotherhood of Man." Not a bad statement, it seems to me, though it has become more elaborate since then. There was Sunday School in the basement afterwards and you might get a gold star for enough attendance.

Dr. Simmons,—so quiet,—luminous, kind, had a military nose and a wide mustache. He was from Wisconsin and famous as a naturalist. Like Wordsworth, he had walked hundreds of miles through the forest. His personal life, I am afraid, was very difficult and sad—a wife always ill, perhaps insane. His daughter was named Echo—long flowing garments, a cloud of pale hair and mysterious grey eyes. I thought she was a dryad, a wood nymph. They had a forlorn little house far, far out south, alone on a moor. Probably it was only as far as Dupont and Lake Street.

My parents loved him dearly and my father wrote: "He is probably better informed about science than anybody in the Northwest ..." and added with ardent admiration, "His discourses show his unabounded admiration for every sincere religious belief."

In Dr. Simmons book "The Unending Genesis" he wrote so tenderly and beautifully about the Book of Genesis—(usually a total absurdity, an asininity to scientists and pedestrian Unitarians.) "Science," he said, "is not so much ruining the old story but enlarging it, replacing its beautiful poetic fancies by showing that its seven days did not end. All the work of the old legend is still before our eyes, not once alone but continually. We are learning to see all around us this more wonderful Genesis."

Being Unitarian children, we were not christened. There were four girls and a boy. They called him "Boy" and didn't bother to name him. Then another boy was born so they had to find a name—Sigurd (The greatest Norse virtue is courage and that is what Sigurd means.) But the next boy was not named for a few years—there was always the effort to find the perfect name. Finally they decided to name him Arnulf. He was old enough to protest. He said he wanted to be named Albert after the policeman's little boy. They explained to him that Arnulf meant Eagle-Wolf. "I'll take it," he said.

To me, about eight years old, the ecclesastical situation was very interesting. I had a passion for English history, especially the legends of Robin Hood. Next to me in the pew there was a very large, stout man with a jolly round face and turned-up nose and quite bald. "Is that Friar Tuck?" I whispered to my mother. No. It was Mr. Hjalmer Quist, she explained.

Another very interesting thing about the Unitarian Church: there were so many fascinating eccentric people, like Mr. Buell, a Single Taxer and vegetarian, and he prodded you in the ribs to see if you wore corsets. He didn't approve of them.

Now my wonderful parents—Did Unitarianism add to their grandeur and wisdom? I think it did. We grew up more lighthearted and untrammeled than Orthodox children, over-awed and inculcated with guilt, (Original Sin.) The hopeless naughtiness of that! Always having to drag Original Sin around! I think we were just as benign and good as the others, perhaps more so—more original, easier laughers, allowed to even have a little engaging rascality.

And my parents were generous to all religions—all of us poor humans groping in the darkness toward Eternity. The only thing wrong about Orthodoxy, they thought, was the grimness, the fraidy-catism, the self-righteous conceit, always trying to discipline others.

I find in a letter my mother wrote to Anne: "Torvald and I were having a little religious conversation and he said, 'Is God a bird?'"

This shows there was not much religious alarm in the family. We never said our prayers and no one told us how. The neighbor children had to say at night that frightening and dismal prayer, "If I should die before I wake . . . ." And it was only when I heard people speak of church and religious and show their distressing tinted cards of Jesus and his disciples traipsing barefoot in their nightgowns, that I became scared of graves, dead bodies, sin and Hell and other horrors, quite unnecessarily.

An interesting thing is that entirely unadmonished I became religious myself, quite cheerfully and naturally so. And whenever great men and women reveal in their lives and works their souls—Tolstoy, Blake, Carlyle, Bach, Michelangelo, Mozart, St. Joan, St. Catherine of Sienna—there expands in me a kind of light and recognition. I seem to see farther into the mysterious gloom— perhaps not so gloomy after all.

My anxiety is that Unitarians will become only Science Idolators. Perhaps God *IS* becoming a bird to them—not a nice live bird but a stuffed bird. An electric bird, a gasahol bird. In fact I like science less and less. Isn't it Intellectual Pride? Maybe it's Lucifer after all. See how they are always measuring and counting, and what's so wonderful about that? Usually it is merely utilitarian and destructive—weaponry and herbicides, shots for cancer that don't work, more computers, more concrete on meadows, faster and more terrible airplanes looking exactly like those fiends that great Dante saw in his genius and appalling imagination. No. Science may be the Tree of Death. Where is the love and beauty in it?

Just the other day in that remarkable periodical that costs 25 cents a year, the Catholic Worker, I discovered that both Dostoevsky and the great Russian theologian Berdyeav said exactly the same thing: "Beauty will save the world."

I believe it. Please remember that and make a note of it.

SPRINGTIME REBELLION

Jean Husby

The day began as usual. A rooster crowed. Birds began to twitter in the trees. Mathilda heard these outside-sounds through the open window. Gunda had always said, "Leave the window open one inch, at least. A little fresh air is good for you." *Gunda knew what was good for you. She was a nurse. She always told you what was good for you and she expected you to listen and heed her words.* Mathilda thought of Gunda—*Gunda was solidly built, like the Hanson side of the family, stocky, square, strong. Ole laughed and said that Gunda was so strong—no, tough, he said—that she would live forever. But she died, like everyone else. Only the weak live to be eighty-eight, like me,* she decided. Mathilda smiled to herself. There was no else to smile at. She was alone—in the big square house. The big square house was quiet, so quiet. Sometimes she thought she heard one of her brothers upstairs. *They must be gone,* she thought. *Oh, they've been gone for years!* The sun came up and touched the flowered wallpaper; a spray of lilacs bloomed in the warm light. Mathilda looked at the calendar hanging on the back of the closed door. *You don't hang calendars on your walls, you know, but you can hang one behind the door. No one will see it.* She felt a satisfaction at having a calendar with big numbers, from the bank, big black numbers, easily seen. *It's April. Twenty-ninth? Thirtieth? Oh well, it doesn't matter. It's April.* Mathilda liked April. She could hear the wind soughing through the pines. In northwestern Minnesota spring can be blustery. *The wind—maybe it is March and I turned the calendar page too soon. No matter.* Mathilda! She thought she heard Gunda call her name. "Nothing gets done if you stay in bed all day," Gunda had always said. Mathilda did not move. *Gunda is not here. She died, in February? She didn't call me—it's just my imagination.* Mathilda thought about force of habit, about getting up when you are called.

She turned over and looked out the south window. *Maybe Halvdan is out there mowing. Nay, Mathilda*—she chided herself. *If this is April there is no hay to mow. I like Halvdan. He is so steady. If I had married I would have married someone like Halvdan. What if I had married?* She looked at the ceiling and imagined herself married to Halvdan. *I would have moved to a different place— instead of spending eighty-eight years on this one.* Irritation brought action and Mathilda sat up, lowered her thin feet to the floor and into her waiting slippers.

The morning routine slowly unfolded. The sun was well up in the sky before Mathilda sat down at the kitchen table for breakfast. She and Gunda had breakfasted together in that dark north kitchen for—always, it seemed. Mathilda had suggested they move to the dining room on the south side of the house, set up a little table right by the bay window and look at the geraniums as they ate. Gunda had vetoed her suggestion. "That takes too much time. Dallying over breakfast is a bad habit to get into," Mathilda picked up her bowl of cereal, walked into the sunny dining room, pulled a chair over to the bay window and gloried in the salmon color of the geraniums.

Is this the day the circle is coming for coffee? Gunda always arranged things, made the plans, assigned tasks. *If we are having circle,* thought Mathilda, *I must get ready. Find the linen tablecloth, the Hardanger one. I hope it is clean and ironed,* she worried. Gunda always said, "We use the best for the Church," Gunda would have bustled around. Mathilda could almost see her getting out the silver service from the corner cupboard. "What's the use of having it if we don't use it." Gunda, who prided herself on frugality, had tried to justify this touch of ostentation. Mathilda thought *Gunda maybe secretly liked being better than the other ladies, having a silver service and using it for circle. Oh no, that is an ungenerous thought.* Mathilda heard the imperious voice, "You must clean the silver service while I drive into town for groceries." She sat by the bay window, forgot circle, forgot Gunda, forgot the silver service, enjoyed the sunlight on the bright blossoms. The sun climbed higher in the sky.

The phone rang. Mathilda ignored it. It rang again. She sighed and slowly walked through the kitchen into the wide front hall. It was her niece. Yes, she was fine this morning. No, it didn't matter if Jen didn't come by today. She needed nothing. Yes, yes, she was in good spirits. She placed the phone into its cradle and sat there, looking out the etched glass of the front door. *It's close in here,* she thought, feeling a touch of claustrophobia. *Should I open the door? Gunda wouldn't like that—letting out the heat.* She opened a drawer and found the key to the door. "We'll keep the front door locked," Gunda had said, "just to be safe." *Who will come in? I have no enemies. Did Gunda have enemies?* She fumbled with the lock. Perhaps she should find the doorstop and leave it only slightly ajar. Not finding the needlepoint-covered brick behind the door, she forgot it and flung the door wide open. The cool spring air rushed in. *Ahhhhhhhhh, it smells so good.*

If we are to have circle, the thought was an anxiety, *I must polish the coffeepot and the teapot, the creamer and the sugarer. Maybe the coffeepot is enough, nobody takes tea—except Mrs. Halvorson.* Mathilda moved into the living room. The mahogany piano on the west wall was flooded with the morning sunlight streaming in from the bank of south windows. Mathilda sat down on the stool. It was too high. She stood and twirled the top clockwise, then seated herself again. On the rack in front of her the old hymnal lay flat and open to "Children of The Heavenly Father". *Page 273,* she noted. *How many times have I said, "Children, turn to page 273. Here is your pitch—sopranos, altos."* Taking the hymnal from the rack she twirled slowly around. She seemed to see in front of her two rows of faces. Together they started to sing, "Children of the Heavenly Father safely in his bosom gather"—Mathilda beat time with her book, moving it up and down in rhythm. She dropped the book to her lap. *All those children, How many years? Thirty? Forty? The children had children.* Names began returning to her—Scandinavian names mostly. She spoke them aloud, giving them their Norwegian pronunciation, "Hjordis, Gudrun, Helga, Eric, Karen, Beret, Ragnhild, Harald." *The children, the children.* Mat-hil-da! Gunda always said, "Save the practicing until evening, after the sun goes down. In the daytime we work." Mathilda replaced the book on the piano and started to get up, thought better of it, moved the hymnbook and found a thin, faded yellow volume from the stack of music on a chair near the instrument. She paged through until she found the piece she wanted. *Mozart, I love Mozart.* Her fingers were stiff but she took pleasure in her playing. The sun reached its zenith.

Oh yes, the silver. She rose, went into the dining room to the corner cupboard, found the tray, the coffeepot, the teapot, the creamer and the sugarer. Deciding to polish them on the dining room table, she set about spreading newspaper over the oak top. *Before I start I'll have a glass of milk.* "You must eat a nourishing meal, Mathilda. If I'm not here you must take the initiative and make a nourishing meal." *Gunda was so bossy. I don't feel like eating—just milk.* Again she chose to sit by the flower-filled window.

A robin hopped across the lawn. *On a nice day like this a little walk would be just the thing. But circle, the silver. Maybe I can take it with me and sit down there by the river while I polish it—and use water from the river to rinse it. A good idea!* She hurriedly found her coat and scarf. Picking up the tray she found it an awkward thing to carry. She needed something to carry it in—*a gunnysack. There's a gunnysack on the back porch.* She found it, put the silver into it, all the silver. Picking it up, she found the sack heavy. She removed the teapot, set it way back in the corner cupboard behind a stack of plates, *where Gunda won't see it. There, that's better. I will go out the back door and across the pasture to the river. It's not far.* When she opened the back door the wide open front door allowed a veritable gale to sweep through the house. She struggled to close the door. *Outside! To feel the sun and the wind! Not to be inside! And the grass is greening.* Skirting the weathered barn she started across the pasture. The ground was wet. Mathilda reminded herself that she should have worn her overshoes, but she didn't want to go back. Down by the river a clump of spring green willows beckoned. *The cowslips are in bloom—what a bright, cheerful yellow. I'm glad I came.* A cow mooed off in the distance. In a few minutes she was as close to the stream as she could get, for the banks were muddy. Finding a downed tree she dropped her load and sat down. Then a clear conception of time came to her. *It must be one o'clock or later. And circle at two thirty. I should not have come. What will Gunda think of me! Well, I better get at the silver.* She opened the sack. No silver polish. No rag. Sometimes Gunda had said, "Mathilda, you are thoughtless." She conceded, *I am thoughtless.*

114

Sitting on the log in the bright sunshine, she felt warm. The wind had diminished to a soft caress. As she took off her scarf one of the hairpins which held her braids caught in the knitted blue wool. She began to take out all the pins. The severe braids which had circled her head fell to her shoulders. She shook them out, running her fingers through them, as she did when she prepared to wash her hair. *How comfortable with no pins. Maybe I should have my hair cut short.*

With no polish to clean the silver, she would have to carry it back, tarnished yet. *Oh no, I can't do that!* She took the ornate coffeepot out of the sack. Idly her fingers traced the pattern on its side. *Mother liked her silver—it was a link to the old country for her.* She lifted the cover and looked in. Then she set it on the log on which she was sitting. It fell off and rolled over near her feet. She took out the creamer. Its feet were especially dark. *They need work,* she noted. *It's so hard to get those feet clean.* She felt the burden of tasks. *To be free of tasks!* She stood up—and then—she did an unthinkable thing! She hurled the silver creamer as far as she could toward the river. It splashed into the water just beyond the willows. The sugarer met the same fate. Mathilda found the action exhilarating, and the tray sailed through the air much farther than Mathilda thought she could throw it, way into the middle of the stream, glinting in the sunlight as it flew. Only the coffeepot was left at her feet. *It, too, might as well go.* She tossed it after its companions. It fell short of the river and landed upright in the mud along the bank. Mathilda picked up the gunnysack, started to fold it neatly, changed her mind, and wadded it into a ball. Just as she tossed it up into the air the wind picked up and caught it, carrying it downstream until it fell in and floated on the water.

The breeze suddenly felt cool. She buttoned her coat, turned and headed back across the pasture toward the barn and house. She walked easily, gracefully, feeling light and free. The fragment of a hymn came into her mind, *nothing in my hands I bring, nothing in my hands I bring.* She held out her slender blue-veined hands. The west wind blew her loose white hair back from her face. The sun shone and a meadow lark sang—just for her.

THE ROMANTIC UNDERTAKER

John Solensten

Dr. Liv leaned back wearily in his own blue dental chair and tried to doze off so he would not be sleepy during the funeral service that afternoon. Sometimes when he became very sleepy at a funeral he would nod off and his head and neck would suddenly go slack. Then he would abruptly jerk his head back and people would turn to stare at him and he would be very embarrassed. If anyone kidded him about it later—and they usually did—he would say, "Why, I guess I plan to sleep at my own funeral too, so why all the fuss?"

Humorous enough, he mused, but he was getting tired of funerals. The entire little town was one large geriatrics ward—one big sunset town. My God! He was 55 and a kind of flaming youth to the ancient widows and widowers living (and dying) there. In some ways it depressed him terribly. Dentistry—the maintenance of decaying teeth, etc. was always a losing, foredoomed proposition. Perhaps that's why dentists so often committed suicide. And then, week-on-week, he saw his own best work... Ugh! Better not dwell on that one. Bury it. Ugh!

The phone rang. Liv groaned, heaved himself up and answered it.

"Hello."

"Hello."

"Who's calling?"

"You don't know? It's me—Olaf Holley."

"Well, sure," Liv said, "—who else."

"Can you come over for awhile?"

"What for?"

"I can't say just now, but come anyway. You don't have a single patient anyway."

"How is it you know that?"

"Oh, I have my ways."

So he had his ways and Liv had no luck trying to sleep so he might as well go to see "Holy Ole," as they called him, over at the Holley Furniture Store, in the back of which (It was a two-faced building with fronts on two parallel streets) was the Holley Funeral Home (Since 1947). The furniture store had a front just like the Our Own Hardware store except that it was painted blue. The funeral parlor had been a bowling alley years back. It had a cement block front painted white except for the Palladian doors Holley had painted ochre so they resembled a glass-paned, eternal and radiant sunrise.

"Yes, sir," somebody in town once said to Liv, "you see, he's got baby cribs on one side and caskets on the other. No wonder he drives two Cadillacs. He's got us coming and going."

"I never thought of that," Liv said, wishing he hadn't *ever* thought about it.

So down main street Liv went, striding along as he always did, with great bounding steps as if he thought with each step, he was going to hop or jump but he usually restrained himself. Of course, when he was drunk he didn't bother to restrain himself and walked like an excited kangaroo or jackrabbit.

"Where you headed, Doc?"

It was Klefsaas the operator of the Mobil Station, the town's practical joker and teller of bad jokes. He stood in front of a grease pit over which a bulbous brown car hunched, spewing black oil into a drain funnel like a humped creature going to the toilet.

"Holley's," Liv said, thinking What the hell business is it of yours anyway?

"Which one?"

Liv shook his head in disbelief. Ah, but the Mayor can't be rude. Liv stepped over toward Klefsaas and leaned into a gas pump. A mistake no doubt. He, Liv, would have to endure at least one bad joke. Death, taxes, bad jokes—all inevitable.

"He didn't say."

"Well," said Klefsaas, stepping closer, his troll eyes dancing in his little round face under the visored cap.

"Yes?"

"I'll say this for Holley ..." Klefsaas said, faking a profound sincerity and shaking his head before poking in one ear for something—something deep.

"Yes?"

"He's just about the last person to let a fella down in this world."

Liv smiled a brittle smile and turned to go. But no use.

"Has the mayor heard about the suits?"

Liv turned back to look hard at Klefsaas. He was smirking his thin frog mouth and wiping his hands on a blackening towel, which, when he hung it down from his belt, said "Property of Fargo Hotel" on the bottom of it in purple letters.

"Suits? What suits?"

"The business with the blue serge suit."

"Oh, that kind of suit?"

"Well, for God's sake, what did you want anyway? What other kind of suit is there except suit suits?"

"Of course," Liv said.

Klefsaas was looking up and down the street and leaning closer to Liv. It was going to be a really dirty joke for sure—something perverted no doubt. Making love to cows? Necrophilia?

"You see," Klefsaas said, "when Mrs. Oren's husband died and Ole had him all laid out, you know what happened?"

"I have no idea," Liv said.

"She turns to Ole and says, 'Oh, I just always wanted him to be buried in a blue serge suit. It would go so nice with his hair and everything, but there's no money for that too.'"

"Yes?"

"'Well,' says Ole, "'I got a fellow found yesterday morning passed on down by the tracks laid out in parlor two. The county bought him a suit—a blue serge by coincidence.'"

"Oh?"

"Well," said Klefsaas, "he showed her the other one and she nearly started bawling. 'It's so nice,' she said, 'but I have to go now to get groceries. All our relatives will be here tomorrow and they like to eat.'"

"She left then?" Liv asked. The car over the grease pit seemed to be staring back at Liv as he looked over at its sad, glaucous headlights.

"I'll get to that. Sure she went, but she felt bad and swung her old Buick around and come back in five minutes or so."

"Five minutes."

"Sure, and you know what she found?"

"No."

"There was her husband in a blue serge suit."

"My gosh," said Liv.

"Just then Ole come in and was beaming all over. ""Oh!"" cries Mrs. Oren, 'my husband looks just wonderful, but how in the world did you do it so fast?'" and you know what Ole said?"

"I ..."

Klefsaas held Liv's arm. He was choking with it all and he looked up the street toward Holley's with gleeful mischief, pressing his frog lips tightly together.

"He said, 'I just switched heads!'" Klefsaas said, choking and pressing the towel at his face.

"Thank you," said Liv, pulling his arm away. "Some joke," he said.

"I knew you'd like it, Doc," Klefsaas said between spasms of laughter.

Liv hurried to get to Holley's, cutting across the street in front of the only car in sight and barely dodging it. Behind him Klefsaas was still choking on his own joke, his face buried in the towel.

Liv stepped into the furniture store. He always preferred to enter there through the beds and end tables and carpet samples—and the baby cribs, of course. Not many were being sold. The whole place was neat and clean and silent as if all the people who used the furniture had departed—"Departed." Liv shrugged his shoulders at the word.

"Dr. Liv, I presume. How infinite in faculties ..."

It was Ole Holley standing there at the corner of a huge oak bed, the post knobs for which were as large as bowling balls.

"This is a special order," he said, nodding toward the bed. "It is in bad taste. They are going to drill finger holes in these and maybe paint them black. They are both nuts from bowling. In fact, they are both nuts you might say but they have oil money from property in North Dakota."

Liv had to laugh, and, while he was at it, laughed at Holley's appearance too. He was a strikingly handsome and dignified 70-year-old man—tall, slim and straight. He looked like a statesman with his black suit and fine moustache and clear blue eyes. He conducted funerals with precision and dignity and great tact. Morticians know the ultimate intimacy, Liv mused—beyond the intimacy shared between bride and groom, doctor and patient. And so ... Yes, he was an impeccable gentleman—a would-be actor when he first went to the University—and then a—a mortician for some reason he had not yet shared with Liv. Perhaps he preferred being a director. Ha! Ha! Liv laughed within himself at his own joke.

"Well," said Holley, "what do you think?"

"The epitome of bad taste," Liv said.

"The what?" Holley was scowling and turing to look into a mirror. He was bending down to look into a mirror—the mirror on the dresser that belonged to the bowling ball bedroom set.

My God! Liv saw that Holley was wearing a toupee. He turned to look at Liv again, his eyes pleading for approval of such daring.

"No, no." he said to Liv, "it can't be that. Besides, it's a gift."

"I meant the *furniture*," Liv said. "I didn't notice the toupee at first. It ... it seemed so natural."

"Really?" Holley said, scowling and turning to look into the mirror again, lowering his shoulders to keep the top of his head level.

"Yes, I mean it."

Holley was smiling then—his smile that comforted—the one he used most often during casket selection Liv recalled. Be generous it smiled.

"It was a beautiful gift," Holley said again, his hands folded together.

"From whom?"

"Come along and you'll see."

Liv found himself being led into the other half of Holley's business—the mortuary. Plaintive French or German 19th century organ music was playing softly through invisible speakers as they walked on deep carpets toward (And Liv gasped, thinking about Klefsaas' joke) room number two.

"Here," said Holley, "is my dear benefactor."

Liv gasped again at what he saw. It was Grace Thorson, a patient—a former patient—from the Luther Memorial Home. It *was* her. Her body lay in studied and silent and waxed and delicately-rouged repose, her hands folded the usual way, her short gray hair stiffly sculptured, her head titled slightly back.

"Doesn't she look like she is waiting for someone?" Holley asked.

"Well ..." Liv began. "She looks ... nice."

"All my girls are beautiful," Holley said, his face set with the zeal of his words, his eyes bright and on the verge of tears.

"Hmmm," said Liv, recalling the rumor that Holley wore black silk suits *all* the time—even during that time when he worked on ... them.

"Touch this," Holley said, bending over to let Liv touch the fine white hair of his toupee.

"Hmmm," said Liv.

"I don't wish to be crass," Holley said, "But I, I had it done in Minneapolis— flew up there and back on the same day."

"Tuesday," Liv said.

"Yes, and I'm so pleased. It's comfortable too these cool days and it's a kind of blessing on my head—her blessing. She played piano. Lovely hands."

"Hmmm," said Liv.

"It won't be long now," Holley said.

"What?"

"The service begins in two hours. You'll be attending?"

"Always," said Liv.

"Well, forgive me, but I have to make a lot of arrangements so I'll have to be going." He paused. "You don't think I'm silly, do you? I hadn't thought of such a thing until she—she offered it. She had a kind of sense of humor. She and I kidded about it. I'm rather severe and formal. It was good to kid. You have your other side, you know, so forgive me if I'm romantic or something in a crazy way."

"What's to forgive?" Liv asked, avoiding the casket with his eyes because he could swear there was a smile lurking *there* somewhere.

"Well," said Holley, shaking Liv's hand solemnly, "... until the service—the farewell, the auf wiedersehen."

"Until," said Liv.

Liv stepped gingerly through the funeral parlor and the furniture store and out into the street. It was getting warm—very warm—out in the noonday sun. When someone opened and closed the front door of the Square Deal Cafe a breath of sour beer and deep fryer grease huffed out at Liv and he hurried back to his office to do some odd chores and, he hoped, to rest a bit.

The funeral service was like all the others he attended at the Lutheran Church. Holley directed the service with panache and great dignity. The hearse (The old wax-slick death buggy) was spotlessly elegant and patient at the curb. Of course, first there was a quick show of the departed, the other old ones leaning toward it to see—whatever they saw. It was all a blank to Liv, a waxen blank. Eyes closed. Nothing there. And yet people were especially kind to one another on those occasions.

He sat quietly in the back row to get as far away from the smells as he could. The odor of the flowers was rank sweet and rich as the perfume of new lilacs, but soon other odors began to come up out of the huge furnace grate on the floor between nave and chancel—to come up from regions of cooking in the church basement: coffee fumes, oily and hot; the unctuous aroma of cold meat sandwiches and hot dishes; the rich, sweet smell of cake and frosting.

Oh, death where is thy frosting? No. Another bad joke, Liv mused.

Liv could visualize them down there in the basement—the women of the Ladies Aide pushing giant blue-black porcelain coffee pots over the yellow-blue flames of the gas-burners; the steaming sinks; the great, fat red arms in the frothing dishwater . . . He could see them because he had seen them *once* and that was enough. He always skipped the funeral feast after that.

"Pssst!" It was Holley, standing there to Liv's left. He had closed the church doors with miraculous silence after everyone was in.

The choir was shrieking an old Norwegian hymn. "I shall be raised up . . . to join the great white host . . ." the old voices cried.

"Barbaric!" Holley whispered, leaning over Liv's shoulder

"What?"

"The smells . . ."

Liv nodded, hoping none of the others heard. He noticed Holley's face was beaded with sweat. Toupee. Improper cooling.

Holley stepped back and stood waiting. He looked terribly dignified standing there.

Suddenly the toupee closed itself up on the top of Holley's head like a giant upside-down tan mushroom and perched there on a bald domain.

Holley felt it immediately, scooped it off into his suit pocket and slipped noiselessly through the church door. Liv got up, went out, stood at the top of the front steps and watched him.

Holley flew down the front steps of the church with four long stiff steps, dashed down the sidewalk to his funeral director's car, tugged open the door and glove compartment and put another toupee on his head. Liv slipped back into church and sagged into his seat. It had all only taken seconds. The Quick and the Dead.

They were ending the hymn and the pastor was mounting the pulpit. In that moment Holley stood next to Liv sitting there at the end of the pew. Liv looked up at him. He was perfectly calm, an elegant gentleman imperially fine and slim and handsome—especially his hair—his fine head of white hair and he wasn't even out of breath. A man in control of his passions.

"This is my spare," he whispered to Liv.

"Hmmm," said Liv.

"She was always a little unpredictable. Always kept you waiting too."

"I'll say," said Liv as Holley slipped noiselessly through the yellow oak doors and went out to wait, like a patient gentleman caller, to take Grace Thorson for a ride in the country.

121

JENNIE

Conrad Simonson

When Jennie sent fattigmann to her children
She packed them in popcorn, having read once
How corn cushions against the slings and arrows
Of outrageous postal clerks. We grew up
Norwegian, eating cardamon-flavored brown
Popcorn. Well, Jennie said, do you want
Fattigmann or don't you: logic like cookies

Jennie loved to sort through those upstairs
Places where she hid the past, finding old
Photographs and report cards, surprising us
With harbored care for what we were and are,
Teaching us to blush. Well, she said, those
Were tender times. Norwegian sentiment still
Surprises us who hide our warmest wants

Jennie abhored a verbal vacuum, tamping us full
With reminiscence, following us to our cars
Like her father before her, who running-board
Hopped his friends goodbye. John and Jennie
Are in our genes, our poetry and talk

Jennie hung tight when the times were mean
Hiding her tears with sudden colds, pretending
To blow her nose in flowered little handkerchiefs

Twenty years Jennie carried children in and out
Of her bending body, a look about her
As if curled down in care, watching them go
Long after they turned last to wave goodbye
Sending birthday and holiday cards with salutations
Penned in and blessings added; sometimes fattigmann

Counting grandchildren, writing their names among
The others for whom she cared in the small book
That smells faintly still of popcorn and cardamon.

IMPRINT

Rita Juul Steinle

For Seamus Heaney

In worn palms
each of them held me hand by hand
as I swung between—
his, like horn, from years of hauling anchor,
the rough tug of spiny rope
that had raised him to Captain of ships
from sail to steam,
now in dry dock from Norway to America.
Hers, red-knuckled
from laundry scrubbed clean
on metal boards
in tubs of scalding water
taken bare.

Fourth of their children and their last,
I was their link
on this excursion
going to the "Amusements" at Palisades Park
but only to stand by
as I found out
when I begged for dimes for the rides
and, like a wound opening toward me,
they cried,
"Men, Mossa, *nei*! Vi kan ikke!
Vi ha ikke *penge*!"
Using "Mossa," my nickname, saying,
"We haven't the money!"

My skin thin even then
each nerve stiff as hairs poking through

I felt for the poverty of their time,
the sting for parents
who had to deny their children
and, humiliated, were cast down.
Pappa's trousers pressed until they gleamed
from wear and Mamma's iron.
She standing tall, starched apron-tied, above the board
as she came down hard,
the iron sizzling.
He grabbing her in affectionate impulse
to leave a pink print on her arm, exclaiming,
" 'pon my word, Christine!
There's not another woman like you!"
And she, in mild protest, crying,
"Aa-ow!"

In my hand
I hold now
their old engagement photo,
printed on hard board,
sustaining it through time—
her wasp-waist pinched in,
brooch clasped at the high throat
of her hand-worked cotton blouse;
fair hair piled on top of the lovely brow.
His stiff collar
and the close crop of his round skull
the barrel chest thrust out,
his gaze level
showing none of the prankishness
that had been his way with us.
The two of them
younger than memory
leaning in toward each other
aching-eyed at the camera
and shining with trust
at the beginning of their long,
luckless years
together.

SEVEN PINES

Steve Swanson

It was far easier to squeeze ourselves out of the college vans
Than from our academic boxes.
We pulled and tugged at jammed-in naugahyde rucksacks
Then walked through brown log doors
Into a space four generations old.
Seven Pines the place was called
(Though only one still stood).
We settled in, began our meetings;
Politely discussed constructionists and formalists
And deconstructionists—while all around us
Were fitted logs, pegged floors, and morticed stair treads.
Hanging on embedded pins above the mantel
Was the very brace of hand-made skiis
That pair of carpenters used to come cross country
Tools on their backs, axes, saws, and all
Ready to begin their quiet century building here
For some small prairie baron
Of iron ore and beef and grain—a mansion—
A wilderness domain of deer and trout.
There was a man who could define the rainbow's end.
Sitting here some 80 seasons later, we poor literature professors—
Still trying to stake our claims by redefining almost anything—
Had very little handle on this place
And spoke a language far more foreign to these spaces
Than the soft Norwegian that those craftsmen spoke
Who carved them here.

MY FATHER'S WEDDING 1924

Robert Bly

Today, lonely for my father, I saw
a log, or branch,
long, bent, ragged, bark gone.
I felt lonely for my father when I saw it.
It was the log
that lay near my uncle's old milk wagon.

Some men live with an invisible limp,
stagger, or drag
a leg. Their sons are often angry.
Only recently I thought:
Doing what you want ...
Is that like limping? Tracks of it show in sand.

Have you seen those giant bird-
men of Bhutan?
Men in bird masks, with pig noses, dancing,
teeth like a dog's, sometimes
dancing on one bad leg!
They do want what they want, the dog's teeth say that!

But I grew up without dogs' teeth,
showed a whole body,
left only clear tracks in sand.
I learned to walk swiftly, easily,
no trace of a limp.
I even leaped a little. Guess where my defect is!

Then what? If a man, cautious
hides his limp,
Somebody has to limp it! Things
do it; the surroundings limp.

House walls get scars,
the car breaks down; matter, in drudgery, takes it up.

On my father's wedding day,
no one was there
to hold him. Noble loneliness
held him. Since he never asked for pity
his friends thought he
was whole. Walking alone, he could carry it.

He came in limping. It was a simple
wedding, three
or four people. The man in black,
lifting the book, called for order.
And the invisible bride
stepped forward, before his own bride.

He married the invisible bride, not his own.
In her left
breast she carried the three drops
that wound and kill. He already had
his barklike skin then,
made rough especially to repel the sympathy

he longed for, didn't need, and wouldn't accept.
They stopped. So
the words are read. The man in black
speaks the sentence. When the service
is over, I hold him
in my arms for the first time and the last.

After that he was alone
and I was alone.
No friends came; he invited none.
His two-story house he turned
into a forest,
where both he and I are the hunters.

MY FATHER AND GARTH MORRISON

Robert Bly

I'll tell you a story about my father. Each year men from south of us—Kansas, Missouri, Arkansas, even Alabama and Tennessee—would move through the country, following the small grain harvest north. They would end up in North Dakota or Canada about late September and would then go home again. My father, since he ran a threshing rig, would hire one or two of these men each threshing season. Sometimes I went with him, and at 6:00 A.M. before the rig had started, we would drive uptown to a small park in which some of the men had slept that night. If he saw a man with a face he liked, he would ask him if he could pitch bundles and drive a team of horses.

On one of those mornings, he hired a man whom I will call Garth Morrison, who had come up from a small town in Missouri. Garth turned out to be a good worker, and he and my father got on together very well. He stayed with us during the week. On Saturday night, the teams put away, he would go to town, and be gone Saturday night and Sunday night. But early Monday morning he would always be back and ready for work.

One Monday morning he didn't show up. My father was puzzled, and at about 9:00 A.M. he put someone else in charge of the rig and drove to town to see if he could find Garth. Asking around here and there, he heard that Garth had been picked up by the sheriff Saturday night. Apparently he had made a date with a waitress at a cafe, who had agreed to let him walk her home. At 11:00 he had gone to pick her up and, probably to his surprise, she did let him walk her home, where she lived with her parents. A few words were exchanged—probably a series of misunderstood signals between a southern man and a northern woman. He slapped her face. She went inside furious and complaining. Her parents called the sheriff. The man was from out of state. The sheriff and the judge had a secret court session the next morning—Sunday morning—having refused all along to let Garth call my father on the telephone, and sentenced him to twenty years at Stillwater prison. By Sunday noon he was on his way to Stillwater. By Sunday night the sheriff was back in town. It was said he always tried to show proof of his vigilance shortly before an election.

My father, once he got the story from the reluctant sheriff, was enraged. He shut down the threshing rig, and with his best friend, Alvin Hofstad, got in the car and drove to St. Paul to see the attorney general of Minnesota. The attorney general agreed that the facts gave off a bad odor. He went with my father and Alvin Hofstad to Stillwater, where they talked to Garth and verified the story. He then had Garth taken out of the prison and returned to the county jail in Madison to await trail. He stayed in the county jail a month or more, and we as boys would go up to talk with him through the window. My father hired a lawyer and paid for Garth's wife and infant son to come up from Missouri for the trial. They stayed with us and she testified at the trial; I remember her holding the baby on the stand. The jury convicted Garth of simple assault, and the judge ruled that the time already spent in jail more than served out the appropriate sentence. He was released and the family returned to Missouri.

My father never spoke to the sheriff again for the rest of the sheriff's life. Garth did not come north again either. The spring following the trial, Garth and his wife invited my father and mother down to Missouri for a visit. They drove down, and it turned out that everyone in that small Missouri town knew the story. When my father went for a haircut, the barber would not let him pay, and whenever he and mother went into a restaurant, the owner would not accept their money.

To be able to respect your father is such a beautiful thing! I learned then that the indignation of the solitary man is the stone pin that connects this world to the next. The more easy-going businessmen in Madison, who had so many friends, would have left Garth sitting in his cell for twenty years. They would have been afraid to put their hand into the web of social friendships, afraid the web would not be repaired over night, or that the spider of loneliness would bite them. I learned too that when you have been unselfish, people respond not in words but by feeding you. I learned so much from that one story! We don't need to read books on ethics or to see documentaries on television; one moral example will do for a lifetime.

131

FOR MY UNCLE PETE,
WHO LOST ALL HIS FARMS

Robert Bly

If we go back, if we walk into the old darkness, we will find
Washington brooding under the long bridges,
the dead still ablaze in the anguish of the egg,
Indian-screams echoing in the compression chambers of shells,
soldiers disappearing into the tunnels inside the flashlight case,
Mexican farmers falling, and soap buried alive.

Anguished beings are alive deep in the history books:
sugarbeets that give blood, stones that migrate
to the sky, leaving tracks among the stars,
drunken ward-heelers crawling in the icy gutters.
American history is the story of something that failed:
the country is a horse-beater with a red moustache
knocked down at last by a horse and bitten.

The history amounts to a wife howling at a husband
to buy more, and buy more land, and later
rationing him to a pint of whiskey and five cigars a day.
It amounts to land pyramided with mortgages and lost,
to some greedy fire burning soddenly in the finger tips,
fingers that turn over pages of deeds, fingers on fire,
fingers that would light the sky if lifted at night.

A RUTABAGA

Robert Bly

The rutabaga is such a squat, fearsome thing—a sort of German observation balloon that observes below the ground. It notices the worms pass on their thundery errands, and during the night watches weird beetles passing outside the cottage.

It is about the size of the testicle of a two-thousand pound bull. The lower half (in its double color it resembles a bobber) is pale dream, a gorgeous deep cream, the undoubtful high forehead of a man of inherited wealth. And the upper half is winered, something urgent, a reckless furtiveness that calls attention to itself, the burglar that wears red clothes, or a hermit sitting high on a pile of rutabagas. The Burgandy color is altered here and there by whitish streaks.

In the hand it rocks in its own cool ocean world. The hand feels complimented by it, as if it had been given a gift: the solid drift of snow that keeps the henhouse warm, or the waves the storm throws against it.

A knife has cut off both taproot and foliage. The cut at the bottom shows the raw flesh, as a severed head shows the neck. Faint rutabaga rings reverberate up into the skull.

When we bite into it, we taste an embittered story out of the Depression, that ends with the whole family scattered, the furniture dispersed, the old pump no longer working, a sour old man camped in the living room, and crusted cans of Carnation condensed milk on the kitchen table. Last night I dreamt that Christmas was coming, and you were in the house practising music upstairs with a young, dark-haired man ... a drummer. Each time you hit the sheet music with your wooden stick end, notes came out. The tune was: "When the Saints Come Marching In."

FINDING AN OLD ANT MANSION

Robert Bly

The rubbing of the sleeping bag on my ear made me dream a rattlesnake was biting me. I was alone, waking the first morning in the North. I got up, the sky clouded, the floor cold. I dressed and walked out toward the pasture. And how good the unevenness of the pasture feels under tennis shoes! The earth gives little rolls and humps ahead of us ...

The earth never lies flat, but is always thinking, it finds a new feeling and curls over it, rising to bury a toad or a great man, it accounts for a fallen meteor, or stones rising from two hundred feet down, giving a little jump for Satan, and a roll near it for Calvin ... I turn and cut through a strip of cleared woods; only the hardwoods are still standing. As I come out into the pasture again, I notice something lying on the ground.

It's about two feet long. It is a wood-chunk, but it has open places in it, caves chewed out by something. The bark has fallen off, that was the roof ... I lift it up and carry it home kitty-corner over the field.

When I set it on my desk, it stands. The base is an inch or two of solid wood, only a bit eaten by the acids that lie in pastures. The top four or five inches is also solid, a sort of forehead.

In between the forehead and base there are sixteen floors eaten out by ants. The floors flung out from the central core are light brown, the color of workmen's benches, and old eating table in Norwegian farmhouses. The open places in between are cave-dark, the heavy brown of barn stalls in November dusk, the dark the cow puts her head into at the bottom of mangers ... A little light comes in from the sides, as when a woman at forty suddenly sees what her mother's silences as she washed clothes meant, and which are the windows in the side of her life she has not yet opened ...

And these open places are where the ant legions labored, the antlered layers awakening, antennae brush the sandy roof ceilings, low and lanterned with the bullheat of their love, and the lively almsgivers go forth, the polished threshold passed by thousands of pintaillike feet, with their electricity for all the day packed into their solid-state joints and carapaces. Caravans go out, climbing, gelid with the confidence of landowners; and soon they are at work, right here, making delicate balconies where their eggs can pass their childhood in embroid-

134

ered chambers; and the infant ants awaken to old father-worked halls, uncle-loved boards, walls that hold the sighs of the pasture, the moos of confused cows, sound of oak leaves in November, flocks of grasshoppers passing overhead, some car motors from the road, held in the sane wood, given shape by Osiris' love.

Now it seems to be a completed soul home. These balconies are good places for souls to sit, in the half-dark. If I put it on our altar, souls of the dead in my family can come and sit now, I will keep this place for them. The souls of the dead are no bigger than a grain of wheat when they come, yet they too like to have their back protected from the wind of nothing, the wind of Descartes, and of all who grew thin in maternal deprivation. Vigleik can come here, with his lame knee, pinned in 1922 under a tree he himself felled, rolling cigarettes with affectionate fingers, patient and protective. And my brother can sit here if he can find the time, he will bring his friend if he comes; my grandmother will come here surely, sometimes, with the ship she gave me. This balcony is like her kitchen to the southwest, its cobstove full of heating caves; and Olai with his favorite horse and buggy, horsehide robe over his knees, ready to start for town, with his mustache; the dead of the Civil War, Thomas Nelson, fat as a berry, supported by his daughters: and others I will not name I would like to come. I will set out a drop of water and a grain of rye for them. What the ants have worked out is a place for our destiny, for we too labor, and no one sees our labor. My father's labor who sees? It is in a pasture somewhere not yet found by a walker.

PHEASANTS

Ole Lokensgard

We thought the pheasant
Hushed in bushes
Near our working,
Hammering, sawing,
Talking, came
For protection,
Thinking cats
Would never think
That he might hide
So close to us.

We took delight
In his cunning and peeked
Occasionally to be sure
He was still there.
He changed positions
Subtly, feathers
Ruffed, wings
Puffed, head
Down. Before
Dinner, we looked

Again and saw
His feathers slumped,
Lumped body,
Wing sprung
Out, splayed
Wry, askew;
And crawling under branches,
We found he had been dying
All the time
Of hidden wounds.

And when my father
Buried him,
I remembered
A Minnesota storm
When he brought home
A pheasant nearly frozen
Who convalesced in cardboard
Until we let him go,
Beating and cawking
Across brittle fields.

BUILDING A SHED ON NANTUCKET

Ole Lokensgard

We race cold
Weather, the high and the thin
Scud of clouds, the cringe
And bleak chatter of choke
Cherry leaves clustering,
Reclustering against nude
Raw sheets of plywood.
Talk is short words.
    (Dark closes in from both morning and night.)

Not knowing exactly
What to do
Next and how make
Progress slow, slow
To a crawl long and drawn
Out as if we sense the city
Like a mirage far across
The wide desert waste
Of sea, calling us
Back to habitual reality,
That customary progression.
    (Seen from a distance, the hammer rings in the air.)

Just before waking
We feel white
Cedar shingles soft
In our roughening hands, cut
Them smooth fitting, read
Their perfect passing like letters
Typed across a page
With no real spaces

Like the pure message of time
As we begin to hear
The tick, seconds, minutes
Of an alter-life,
And as the dreams evaporate like water
We slip into bodies-
What is it we really do?-
And wonder at the feel of this life,
Persona of the aching muscles.
    (Hose: water cupped in the parentheses of hands).

The day comes and goes
In primary colors. The spectrum
Of pride etches the finishing
Touches with relief, half
Moons in primed pine,
Over-confident stumbling
Which we decide
Shall be considered
Those deliberate errors
Built into our cathedral
As a sign, a message to the all
Mighty of the extent, here and
Now, of our control.
    (We were so careful, she said, on what doesn't show.)

RIVER

Ole Lokensgard

In comforts of heat, earth smells.
Water brought the dust alive.
The welcome humor of the rain
Restored the secret river's strength.
Water calming after storm
Reflects the rainbow to a circle.

A puff of silt—a crayfish freezes.
Fragments settle on its shell,
A pebble cluster in the mud.
Current puckers darkened ridges
Against the drying caps of granite.
Underwater, stones are moving.

Emerging turtles dry on logs.
Always hungry, horseflies mumble.
In cottonwoods, cicadas shrill.
A dragonfly suspends itself,
Still, then blurred, a dash of green
That disappears against the sumac.

Live clams trench the depths
To puzzles. High on sandy banks,
A rainbow shell of pearl dries slowly,
Cupping water in its ear,
Water stilling idle rumor
Of other world and lisp of ocean.

IV. GOING BACK:
THE LAND AND THE MEMORY

THE MOTIVES—AND COMPULSIONS—for Norwegian immigrations to America have been studied and carefully listed by a number of historians, including Arlow W. Anderson in his The Norwegian-Americans *(Twayne Publishers). The motives for going back—for seeking out the places from which many Norwegian-Americans derived their family names—the Ulvestads, the Hovlands and others—are more difficult to focus.*

And yet there seems to be a deep and essential connection between the two movements—one permanent, usually; the other of shorter duration (the good relatives feeding the Norwegian-Americans excellent breakfasts and patiently helping them practice the language with the merest soupcon of a smile now and then).

Writing in a 1929 issue of American Magazine *O.E. Rolvaag said, "The vast wilderness of the Middle West could not, at least at that time, have gained much momentum had it not been for the romantic mood which about the year 1800, began to gain sway of men's minds in the nations of the North." In* The Norwegian-Americans, *Arlow W. Anderson notes that, "Apart from mainly economic considerations, a mysterious desire for movement characterized the nineteenth century in the Northern lands "and that, "The rise of national leaders among poets and peasants spread a romantic veil over the country."*

Perhaps it is this "romantic" desire to know—to seek out—that comes full cycle in understanding what it is to be Norwegian-American in a very personal way. For to know one's parents and grandparents—that first generation of immigrants to the New Land—it is helpful to see the people and places imaged in their memories—people and places lovingly catalogued in a 19th century Norwegian immigrant song:

> *Farewell, valley that I cherish,*
> *Farewell, church and trees and home,*
> *Farewell parson, farewell parish,*
> *Farewell, kith and kin, my own ...*

The impulses for going back to see "the old country" are, as the following pieces reveal, a curious blend of the practical and the romantic. Perhaps Norwegians need an excuse to be sentimental. And, of course, sometimes the "going back" is only an imaginary journey—an imaginative process of trying to perceive what the immigration was like—a sharing of feelings, a communion of hope and despair.

REMEMBERING IN OSLO THE OLD PICTURE OF THE MAGNA CARTA

Robert Bly

The girl in a house dress, pushing open the window,
Is also the fat king sitting under the oak tree,
And the garbage men, thumping their cans, are
Crows still cawing,
And the nobles are offering the sheet to the king.
One thing is also another thing, and the doomed galleons.
Hung with trinkets, hove by the coast, and in the blossoms
Of trees are still sailing on their long voyage from Spain;
I too am still shocking grain, as I did as a boy, dog tired,
And my great-grandfather steps on his ship.

FOR NATIVE NORWEGIANS BORN AFTER ME

Rita Juul Steinle

I remember the year when you were born
when my aunts, streaming long black coats
like the frantic seabirds that circled our wake,
flew here and there to find me
then carry me kicking from the door
I had crept like a crab through
into the Men's Room on the *S.S. Bergensfjord*
bucking heavy seas and bound for Norway.

I remember the departure at the dock in Brooklyn
with everyone singing
"Ja, Vi Elsker Dette Landet"
and "Oh, Say can you See ... ?"
Red, white, and blue flags of each country waving;
handkerchiefs dabbing watering blue eyes
then signaling a wan farewell.

I remember the ship pulling out, we standing
at the railing.
Bands on the pier kept playing
the dock receding
someone holding me, probably Mama,
then passing the huge Lady of Liberty
her size to cause shivers,
the skyline of Manhattan left behind.

Dreams through the years evoke that early memory
of unsteady decks awash and creaking;
the bow charging through rocking seas
ill-natured and frightening.
Wood and water, sloping.
The sound of many feet running.

Being part of a stream of driven people running.
A night quality of darkness.
Feeling trapped.
There are houses. Walls are ultramarine—
wet as well as black.
Up and down we run around buildings
the ground uneven,
looking to hide, feeling surrounded.
The enemy in uniform, perhaps German.
They seem to be closing in.

OF BREAD AND SHADOWS, BEGINNINGS

Brenda O. Daly

I was cleaning out my mother's sewing closet when I came upon a faded letter from my Uncle Olaf. It had been stuffed, incoherently, into a box of family photos that would, someday, be arranged in an album. It must have been about 1959, shortly before I went off to college, that I sorted through these fragments of family history, trying to piece together the stories that define me. I could locate my mother's story. She had grown up on a North Dakota farm that I had visited often, but my father's story—which began in Norway—seemed shrouded in shadows, as vague and confused as my mother's sewing closet.

My mother laughed when I read Uncle Olaf's letter to her. When he described the dangers of baking bread—smoke stinging his eyes so badly he could scarcely see to write—my mother recalled Grandma Turi's kitchen. "I used to love going to your Dad's house after school," she said. "There was always fresh bread just coming out of the oven, and we could eat it hot. At my house we weren't allowed to do that." I tried to picture my mother as a school girl, talking and laughing in Grandma Turi's kitchen, eating the hot bread, forbidden in her house. I once dreamt of my grandma's bread. In the dream I could hear a minister's somber, droning voice, but the smell of baking bread made me wildly impatient. I wrested the podium away, flung open the top, and there, inside, was the hot bread. The dream ended as I broke off large chunks of bread to share with the congregation, my own variation upon, "Give us this day our daily bread."

My mother had memories of Grandma Turi's kitchen in North Dakota, but I remembered only her kitchen in Minnesota. We had gone there for a summer holiday—probably in 1953—for I was old enough then to understand what a country called "Norway" was. When my grandmother opened her trunks from the old country, I could at least place Norway on a map, though it would remain—for many years—like a dark continent in my imagination. It may have been my father's drinking that made me associate Norway with something shadowy and vaguely shameful. I knew that my alcoholic grandfather had gone back to "the old country," abandoning his family in the United States. The only trace of Norway that remained was a curious lilt in my grandmother's voice and her habit of saying "yellow" when she meant "jello," which made everyone laugh. The old country, I thought, must be something embarrassing, like saying

146

"yoke" when you meant "joke."

But in the summer of 1953, for the first time, I began to feel a certain pride in this Scandanavian past. For despite the Great Depression and World War II that had broken up the family, my grandmother had managed to establish a real home at last. And during that summer her kitchen offered me a kind of warm, orderliness that I could understand. If I did my work in the morning, I was free to play in the afternoon. Her praise warmed me, like the summer sun. No one, she said, could clean a stove as well as I did! In the back yard, where my sister and I played, wild strawberries grew everywhere, even under the clothes line, where we sometimes crushed them during our games. Ivan and Sigmund, my grandmother's youngest sons, would go off to work, but Olaf stayed behind, entertaining us for hours with improvised games. One of them was called, simply, "The Bee." He would give us each a quarter, he said, if we could sit perfectly still while he played the bee—buzzing, buzzing, buzzing, ever closer to our eyes, our ears, our noses. Our greatest delight was losing the game, squirming deliciously, twitching, trying not to twitch, and finally bursting into unrestrained laughter. Olaf could always make us laugh. "I have a car," he said, "called a Rolls Kanardly. It rolls down one hill and can hardly get up the next." Though I did not know it at the time, he would never drive again. He was gradually going blind from scarlet fever contracted in his childhood.

One morning my grandmother woke me very early. She wanted to take my sister and me for a walk, she said. Her grip tightened as we walked along the road, a dirt road lined with wild blue flowers. Ivan, she told us, had died during the night. Blond, Norwegian Ivan, her youngest son, was dead. We still have photographs of him taken that summer, a strikingly handsome man who lifted my mother up in his arms, whirling her around in a welcoming dance. Only a few days before his death someone had taken us to see him at work in the iron ore pits outside Hibbing, Minnesota. In an old photograph he stands beside a stunningly large truck, a machine so huge that its wheels are twice as tall as my uncle. I recall him leaping into the cab and driving the truck down a spiraling road into the bottom of the pit. There he disappeared, as if swallowed by the ant-size truck which might, itself, disappear into the scarred earth. Tax money from the pit, someone said, had built Hibbing High School where my uncles went to school.

But now Ivan was dead. At his funeral the church was filled with people, many of them young, some of them pretty girls in summer dresses, crying at the back of the church. We sat in front. In the midst of the sermon my aunt Kari stood up, shouting at the minister, "That's a lie. That's a damn lie!" I'm sure my father was angry, but this was a public place, and he pulled her down gently. I heard, later, that they had sent Kari away somewhere because she was mad. Did they send her to a madhouse? Is that what they did to you if you got mad?

On the day of Ivan's funeral, my grandmother served a family dinner, opening her trunks from Norway to prepare for this rare occasion. How she must have worked and saved and planned for this family gathering, and now there was an irreparable hole, the place Ivan would have sat. From her trunk my grandmother took finely stitched linen towels and tablecloths, and the few remaining pieces of silver. Most of her silver had gone to a grocer during the Depression, she told me. They had always meant to buy it back. Among the remaining pieces was a gravy ladle that had been her mother's. I have it now, as well as her black wool folk costume, lavishly embroidered in bright colors. She had done all this fine needle work during the winter of her sixteenth year, she said, just before her sister and father died from the plague. I could see places in the wool that had been mended to disguise the moth holes.

Ivan's funeral dinner, a ceremonious occasion so carefully prepared by my grandmother, ended in a fight. It began with words between my father and my aunt Kari. I didn't understand why he wrestled her to the floor. I thought my aunt Kari an exotic creature, a slim worldly woman who had traveled all the way from New York. Her purse was filled with fascinating objects—lipsticks, jewelry, keys, perfume. In a photograph from that time she stands beside a man's convertible, the first I had ever seen. She is leaning slightly against the car, an elegant pose, I thought, and wearing a white dress that falls gracefully over her slim hips. The shoulders are padded, accentuating her narrow body; across her midriff is a dramatic vertical splash of brown that matches her hair. Was it about this time that my grandmother had intercepted her love letters? Kari was angry, my mother told me. In high school she had been a hot-headed girl, an aggressive basketball player, swift and courageous, my mother's best friend. Unlike my mother, Kari never married and, though she has become what people call "an old maid," there was plenty—it seems to me—to make her mad.

Madness and war, depression and anger—these psychological states mingle with historic events, with holes in the family fabric. In a recent letter my grandmother told me: "*Depression hit Norway fast, both on See and land. Jorgen lost out on everything. Famers and buisness suffered loss, and went Bankrupt nearly half of them. Jorgen had been in USA. before, so he planned on go back and make some money. He leaft Norway for Canada in 1925 in july. He found out he could not make mony as planned and sent a ticket to me and children. We leaft Norway in july 1926.*" The depression she mentions here came before World War I, and I have often wondered—given the many stories of depressions, plagues, and wars—how she found time for gayety of any kind. Yet she has told me of her courtship, of how Jorgen drove a motorcycle, of how she rode in the sidecar, of how her father didn't approve. My grandfather does look like a romantic figure through her eyes, and I have seen the medals he won in ski races. As a girl, my mother told me, she used to see him from her kitchen window, walking to town. "He was so graceful," my mother said, "even his walk was like a dance." But dancing must have ended soon for my grandmother.

She would swiftly become a migrant mother. At the age of 27, she was on her way to the U.S. with four children: my father, Jorgen, age six; my aunt Kari, age five; Olaf, three; and Guinhild, one. Her letter continues, "*When Jorgen and Kari started school in USA they could not speak or understand English. We all spok Norwegen at home, but 3 months of school they only spoke English betwen self and the younger ones. After one winter in school the Teatcher said J. was ihead of his class. If it was somting he did not understand he came right up to her and asked she said."* Though a mother's view of her son may not be entirely trustworthy, my father always did seem to me a man of words. He did not go to college—he went off to war instead—and I have often thought of him as an artist who, lacking an art form, became dangerous.

Shortly after my sister and I were born, when we were too young to remember him, he became a sailor. I considered him a stranger, a man whose return I associated with a large pair of boots that appeared, mysteriously, in our living room. According to my mother, I informed him immediately and decisively, "This is *my* mother." The arrival of this intruder—a man sleeping with my mother—is vaguely connected to other changes: the disappearance of an old red piece of cardboard, marked "Ice," from our window, and the new "frigidaire" in the kitchen. Then there was a voice on our radio, apparently some years later, that kept exclaiming about a man who kept getting more and more boats. I recall being bewildered by a man who, like my father, seemed so enchanted by boats, but someone must have corrected me: not "boats," but *votes*. The war had ended, my father's sailor suit had been put away long ago, and Harry Truman had been elected President of the United States.

In 1949 we had moved to North Dakota where "home" would change into an unarticulated war between my mother and father. Was it my father's drinking, or my mother's frequent pregnancies, or the combination of both, that made home so oppressive? Whatever the cause, it was a great relief to spend a summer at Grandma Turi's in 1953. We had left my father behind in North Dakota; therefore, I had both my mother and grandmother to myself. They worked and laughed together, and I could ask my Grandma Turi to tell me stories. Sometimes she would tease me with, "I'll tell you a story about Jack and Nory, and now my story's begun. I'll tell you another about her brother, and now my story is done." But when I asked her if she liked to read, as I did, she answered solemnly, "After the children were born, I gave it up. I was afraid I might lose track of them, afraid they might be hurt." Once, she said, my father—her first-born—had gotten away from her, and from that time forward she would allow herself to read only one book, the Bible. Even on board the ship, she said, Jorgen had wandered off. Her brother found him, but they had feared he was lost at sea. And with that she pressed her lips together tightly, closing the subject.

Some years later, during a visit to my mother's family farm, my sister and I would walk daringly up the road to where my father once lived. On the other side of the hill, we had been told, was the old mine where Grampa Jorgen had earned a living, at least for a time, during the Great Depression. Near the mine was an old tarpaper shack which, in 1926, my grandfather had tried to prepare for his wife and four children. He had made an attempt to paper it and, according to Grandma Turi, the wallpaper *was* pleasing, though it had been hung in the wrong direction. I tried visualize the paper. Did it have flowers that went sideways, rather than upright? Had my grandfather been drinking when he hung it?

Finally, like two young Nancy Drews, my sister and I would investigate the old North Dakota homestead. I posted myself as a look-out on the road while my more courageous sister went forward to knock on the door. Only a skunk responded, sauntering brazenly around the house behind her. We fled. Here was the place we had heard so much about, the place where Grandma had baked the bread, the kitchen where so much laughter and talking—at first in Norwegian, then in English—had attracted my mother.

It looked grim to my sister and me, even in the sunlight. Later we would learn why the family had left. According to my grandmother, a serious accident in the mine caused my grandfather continual pain. That's why he had "taken to drink." A doctor had performed crude surgery, cutting an "X" in my grandfather's skull—on the pressure point—and folding back the flaps of his scalp to explore. Alcohol had been the only anaesthetic available. After this operation, he suffered so much that he could no longer work. My mother's father survived the Depression, expanding his farm to more than 3,000 acres, but Grandpa Jorgen had lost everything, again. This time the family broke up for good. Because he was the oldest, my father was chosen to kill the family dog, a German shepard named "Beauty." The older children would go to work on farms, the younger children would go with Grandma Turi to Hibbing, where she would become a housekeeper. No one would take Beauty along. Many years later, when he had children of his own, my father bought another German shepherd. We call her "Beauty."

Just how much of Grandmother's story is literally true, I do not know. But it is a fact that my grandmother went to work for a wealthy woman in Hibbing. Her name, appropriately enough, was "Mrs. Class," and she was so fussy that no one could please her. She inspected my grandmother's work with white gloves before pronouncing it "good." But she was kind enough to allow my Grandma to keep her two youngest children, Sigmund and Ivan, with her. It was blue-eyed, blond-haired Ivan who pleased Mrs. Class most, who became like a "grandson" to her. She became so fond of him that she even considered making my grandfather a generous donation for a home. Why did that never happen? Apparently she believed that my grandfather would somehow use the money for drink. Now that I have seen my grandmother's home in Norway, her fine linen and silver, and her wedding photograph—where she is dressed in a gown trimmed with ermin—I often wonder how she felt about coming to the U.S. Her story seems to reverse the usual "rags-to-riches" immigrant tale. As a child, she had known what it meant to have a secure place—a history, a family, a tradition—but as a citizen of the United States she had lost all this without gaining anything in return.

But there were to be even more losses. For suddenly, after World War II had begun, the family would learn that they were not, in fact, "citizens of the United States." An old Hibbing newspaper from this period records the case of a certain "high caste" Norwegian family threatened with deportation. They had come from Canada, according to the news story, entering the U.S. illegally—apparently not long after the law had been changed to prevent such border-crossings. In 1940, when Germany had invaded Norway, the family might be forced to return. Sigmund and Ivan were safe, having been born in the U.S., and my father was safe, having just married my mother, a legal citizen. Everyone else, as it turned out, would be safe because they were "high caste," according to the sympathetic reporter. Obviously, they were not "high class," but *high caste* did mean, at least, that they were Northern European, members of a "pure" race! It is ironic that, though Hitler's racist logic would spare them, my father was prepared to fight for "his" country, against Hitler. He joined the navy, leaving my mother behind to care for my sister and me. Another irony is that this was the most peaceful time in my childhood. American history books, of course, rarely record the experiences of women and children.

For German, Japanese, French, Norwegian, and others, World War II—from the point of view of women—would look very different indeed. During my childhood, war was defined for me by photographs and Oriental artifacts. In one picture my father is standing with two Chinese women. They are smiling. Perhaps this photograph was disturbing to my mother for, when she saw it, she moved on quickly to a photo of her in an Oriental robe. She is standing in the sun light, drying her long brown hair. It reminded her of walking on the North Dakota prairie with her grandmother, Mary Martha, she said. After washing their hair, they would walk together, talking as the sun and breeze dried their flowing hair. My father is conspicuously absent from this scene, as he is absent from the early years of my childhood. Once, on seeing a film with Frank Sinatra in a sailor suit, I thought, "So that's what sailors do!" My father was a slender man who looked, to me, like a boy always leaving for somewhere, and I pictured him—across the sea—dancing in his navy whites. Among the strange objects he brought back from China was a Buddha, carved in rosewood, that still sits on my mother's bookcase. The Buddha's legs are crossed in a lotus position, and his fat stomach protrudes obscenely. I could never understand how anyone could be enticed to worship *him*.

The stave churches of Norway, I would discover many years later, bear an eerie resemblance to Oriental architecture. When my father died in 1976, at the age of 56, he asked that his ashes be buried in his father's grave plot in Norway, and I finally travelled with him to a land across the sea. My grandmother went with us—three of her grand-daughters—for the funeral. From Kristiansand, where her sisters, Theresa and Milla lived, we drove north into the mountains in July. Although my grandmother's brother had remained in the mountains, the family homes were now occupied by strangers. Yet in the grave-yard surrounding the church, I found family names everywhere. And a sign on the mountain road, the place name, was my father's family name. Perhaps my father had never felt truly American, I thought. Maybe he *had* been lost at sea. My ruminations were interrupted by the arrival of a traveling minister, wearing a brown clerical shirt—with traces of his breakfast clinging to the fabric—and carrying a small suitcase from which a sock protruded. For his funeral sermon he changed into more formal attire, a black gown with a stiff white ruff that circled his throat. By then I had learned just enough Norwegian to understand his image for my father's life: a great circle, a return home. The words did not anger me for, after all, my father had been born in Norway and baptised in this very church.

Yet, I thought, the words and attire belonged to another era, to a time and a place that did not include me. If a man's life is a circle, where does that leave his children? Inside, or outside? We had no place in the family cemetary, nor would we ever and, though I felt no need to shout, "That's a damn lie!," what I liked in the church were the colors, not the words. They were strong and rich. The white altar cloth reminded me of Grandma Turi's table linens, and the trimming, painted in gold and rust, was like lacquered Oriental furnishings. The columns of the altar rose to a peak that, painted in shades of blue-green, seemed to move like a horizon of earth and water. I brought back from Norway a bread board that my uncle had painted in the same urgent colors, following a traditional rosemaling pattern, obviously the work of an amateur. It isn't the traditional pattern that delights me, but these stirring desires to find an art form. He had completed the work one winter, Olaf said, when he had injured his foot while chopping wood.

We would not stay long enough in Norway to experience winter, though I felt its chill in the cold mountain steams and in the night air. All of Norway was on holiday, it appeared, soaking in the sun, picnicing, and—in the cities— shopping in open-air markets. During a picnic in the mountains, I saw another illustration of Uncle Olaf's domestic art. After cutting a square piece of birch from a tree, he punched holes along two sides with his knife, shaped it into a cylinder, and sewed the sides together with weed. Then he dropped a circle of birch bark into the cylinder, forming a bottom to complete his basket. While Aunt Milla boiled water for our tea—hanging the kettle from a bough over the fire—we gathered blue berries in the birch basket. From the trunk of her car, Milla brought out a small wooden folding table, placing fresh, home-made bread and tea cups on the tray. How good the food tasted! In my travel journal, I recorded the Norwegian songs she taught us together with descriptions of our stay in Stavanger, Kristiansand, and Oslo.

In Olso, just before leaving for the U.S., we became bona fide tourists, even seeing the obligatory Viking ship. On the horizon, looming above Oslo, I could see a giant ski run, abandoned during the short summer. But as we walked in the famous sculpture gardens, I felt that winter might arrive before our departure. During our final night in Norway, a hotel band played a song popular that summer: "Let your love flow like a mountain stream." My cousin, Jostein, did not quite approve of this imitation American disco music, but a great many Norwegians seemed to enjoy it. They danced, some of them quite drunk, with Bacchanalian abandon, late into the night. My father, I thought, like his father, had loved to dance, but now his ashes lay in the cold mountain earth. While he lay dying in the U.S., I remember my grandmother, kneeling to pray by my father's bed. He had gestured impatiently for her to rise, perhaps rejecting her Madonna-like position.

I am still trying to piece together my father's story, seaming together the official public Norway that I saw in 1976, with more shadowy fragments. "There's more than one version of the Heidi story," he said, as he lay dying, talking out of his dreams. One photograph remains from his childhood in Norway. He is holding the hand of a little girl his age, standing with her in the tall grass. They look old enough to talk, but not old enough to stray from their mothers. Did this boy leave a part of himself in Norway, as his wish to be buried there suggests? Did he want an intimacy with his father in death that he had never had in life? Or did he want to escape the sorrow he had left behind—the shadows he cast upon his children? Before my father's funeral in the U.S., my youngest sister kept playing a song that began, "All my sorrows, all my joys, came from loving the thieving boy." At his funeral in Norway, she wore a peasant skirt and a thin black shawl, as if she were his grieving widow.

That night, as she sat stiffly on the edge of her bed, she reminded me of a painting by Evard Munch called "Puberty." A young woman sits naked on the edge of her bed, her body casting a shadow in the dazzling spring sunlight. I told her, "You can let go now. He's dead. He doesn't need you anymore." My father's story—which is also mine—is not a circle that closes neatly. It still casts a shadow.

LETTERS FROM A NORWAY FARM

Liese Greensfelder

When I was 20 I had a plan to spend three years travelling around the world. I wanted to learn all there was to know about traditional farming methods, for I hoped to some day work as an agricultural advisor in developing countries. I planned to start in Europe, and then move south and east to Africa, Asia, and then home. I hoped to find farming families in rural communities who could provide me with room and board in exchange for work. The $1,200 I had saved at my job in a bakery was going to pay travel expenses from country to country.

The problem was how to get started. I had lived most of my life in Mill Valley, California, a town just north of San Francisco, and although I was an ardent outdoorswoman, I had no previous farming experience, nor any connections in domestic or foreign farming circles. So when I heard of an Oslo based organization that arranged "working visits" for foreigners on Norwegian farms, I sent away for more information. The Norwegian Committee for International Youth Work and Understanding (wisely enough, the Committee refers to itself simply as the "NIU") finds summer jobs for people between the ages of 18 and 30, to "live and work as a member of a Norwegian farm family." This seemed like an especially appropriate place to start my international study of traditional farming, because, two years before, I'd spent a year in Denmark on an American Field Service scholarship, so I knew something about Scandinavia and I spoke fluent Danish, a language closely related to Norwegian. Also, I had heard that in contrast to Denmark's large farms and modern agricultural technology, farms in Norway were small and farming methods traditional. I figured that I could develop muscles and endurance on a Norwegian farm in a somewhat familiar culture before moving down to Spain or Africa to work in a much more demanding and exotic environment.

I received a prompt response to my application informing me that I was to work at the farm of Johannes Hovland, a 60 year old bachelor farmer who lived on his sheep farm near the town of Øystese on the Hardanger Fjord, 50 miles east of Bergen. Another NIU recruit, a young woman from England, would work at the farm at the same time as I.

In April, 1972, I bade my parents and four brothers and sisters goodbye and set off on my adventure. After travelling across the United States and on to Ice-

land, Luxembourg, and Denmark, I reached Norway on May 17. A surprise was in store for me when I arrived in Øystese, as a result of which I spent the next two and a half years in Norway and never did make it further south or east. It is this surprise that is the subject of the letters presented here.

Before I left home, my dear and worried mother had elicited a promise that I would write to her once a week. She saved all my letters, and these letters have now become the basis for this narrative.

Dear Family,

I've arrived safely on Norwegian soil but I've begun to wonder if Norwegian soil is safe. The day I arrived, May 17, turned out to be a great national holiday here in Norway—in commemoration of the end of German occupation after World War II? the King's birthday? constitution day? ... I was too timid to ask anybody what it was; I didn't want to offend a Norwegian with such an ignorant question on my very first day in the country.

I arrived in Oslo at 6:00 a.m. and watched crowds in the country walk up and down the main street all day long. In the morning there was a parade of thousands of children, all waving the red and blue Norwegian flag and singing or playing instruments. In the afternoon, the cafes that served beer were opened and soon a parade of drunken men replaced the children. I've heard that Norwegians enjoy a hearty draught of good Norwegian beer, but this fondness for their native brew seemed to go beyond *that!* Half the men in the streets seemed to be drunk or tipsy. I've never before been grabbed at by so many men in my life! On the other hand, those people who were sober were much more reserved and quiet than a crowd of people back home on the Fourth of July would have been.

Right now I'm in the mountains on the night train between Oslo and Bergen. At this altitude everything is still covered with snow and ice. I feel as if we've all been transported to a silent, frozen planet. Pines and leafless birch trees are sparsely scattered between the boulders of these barren mountains, and here and there churning rivers have broken through their icy mantles.

I can't sleep on trains, and I couldn't sleep on the boat from Copenhagen last night, either. At six a.m. I've got to switch trains at Voss. From Voss there's a train to Granvin and from Granvin I'll catch a bus to Øystese, arriving there at nine a.m. By then I'll have missed two nights sleep. Johannes will wonder what sort of help he's hired when he sees me in this exhausted condition. When I phoned him from Copenhagen, I *think* he said that he'd come with the horse and buggy to Øystese to meet me! Do you suppose he doesn't have a car or tractor?

Same day 4:00 p.m.

What a shock—upon arriving in Øystese I was met by an elderly, heavy-set man who jabbered excitedly in a language I assumed to be Norwegian, but could as easily have been Swahili, for I understood not a word. I was confused; he didn't seem to be Johannes. And a sinking feeling of dismay struck me when I realized I couldn't understand this language. He kept talking and didn't give me a chance to ask him to slow down a little. I was beginning to wonder just who this fellow was when another man and a woman came up to us and with barely a nod of their heads to this gentleman led me away with them to their house just down the road. They spoke the same language I had just been hearing but a little more slowly and clearly so I was able to pick out many Danish-related words. Johannes was in Voss, they told me. This seemed strange. If he were in Voss, why hadn't he come to the train station to meet me? They explained why, and though I didn't understand, they sounded so sincere and logical that I figured his excuse was legitimate. The woman, fru Evanger, made a huge breakfast of bacon, eggs, toast, openface sandwiches, and milk for me. I asked when Johannes was coming home. They said they didn't know. Did they have any idea? Today? Tomorrow? Oh no! not for a few weeks or maybe even months. It was only then that I realized that something was terribly wrong. I asked if Johannes was sick. "Yes, for Heaven's sake! He had a stroke two days ago and is lying quite ill at the hospital in Voss." I guess they'd said this several times before, but this was the first time I'd understood. I suddenly felt very alone and very unsure of myself. What could I do now—where would I go? And what was going to happen to Johannes's farm? Herr and fru Evanger sat down and tried to explain the situation so that I could understand. There were jobs in the hotel here in Øystese or in a near-by nursery if I wanted them. As for Johannes's farm, well, nobody seemed to know about that. He lives alone, and for the time being neighbors are taking care of the animals, but they can't keep that up forever. It is a difficult situation for both Johannes and me.

After breakfast, the Evangers offered to drive me to Johannes's abandoned farm. I wish you were here to see how beautiful it is! From Øystese, a dirt road wound three miles uphill all the way to the farm. We drove through forests of birch, aspen, and evergreens growing between small sheep farms whose deep green meadows were scattered with hundreds of different wild flowers and plants. At the very end of the road was Johannes's farm. It was lovely—the house was wooden, painted red and white, and the barn was made of stone and wood. In the barn were two cows and a calf, a few sheep and a ram. There was a horse, as I had hoped, and she and fifty sheep, each followed by one or two frisking lambs, were grazing in the fields around the house. The sheep in the barn, the Evangers explained, had not yet lambed. The beauty and serenity of that farm so struck me that I've been daydreaming about living there alone. Perhaps I could do some of the work for Johannes.

We talked to some neighbors on the way up and they said that with occasional help from them, I might be able to get along. But it's impractical—I have no idea how to do anything and there's bound to be lots of work that I'm not strong enough or skilled enough to do. Living alone would be sort of scary, too.

Back at the Evanger's, we phoned the NIU in Oslo and told them about the situation. They said that they would get in touch with the English girl who is supposed to work here also, and try to find another farm for her. They know of a farm where I may be able to work back in the eastern part of Norway. After talking to the NIU the Evangers took me to the employment office in Øystese. The man there was helpful and repeated that I could work in the hotel if I wanted, but I know I couldn't stand working indoors all summer. He said he'd try to find a farm for me to work on, but that the prospects weren't too good.

A few hours later he phoned, though. He told the Evangers that the owner of a large fruit farm on the other side of the fjord needs a farmhand. All the work will be outdoors, the wages are good and I'll live as a member of the family. It's a nice family, they say, so I couldn't hope for anything better. Yet, I've been thinking all day long about Johannes's beautiful little farm up in the mountains and what's going to happen to it. The Evangers say that there isn't anyone else in Johannes's family who could take over the farm for him now, so its future is very uncertain. Being up there was like stepping back a hundred years in time. It was so calm, still, and isolated. There weren't any cars or machinery to be seen and the neighbors said that the horse is an honest to goodness work horse and is used for all the heavy work. I don't think that the farm across the fjord has any animals at all.

All this has happened just since this morning and I'm exhausted now. Haven't had any sleep for 48 hours and this day has been terribly long and confusing. Must go to bed, even though it's only six o'clock.

Next evening May 19th

More surprises—when I came down to breakfast this morning fru Evanger told me that her husband had been to Voss last night and that he'd spoken with Johannes. Johannes was very upset about the trouble I'm going through and wanted to talk to me. So this afternoon Ola Maeland, a brother-in-law of Johannes's, drove me to Voss. It was hard to get a good impression of Johannes, because he's so weak from the stroke and his left side is paralyzed. He seemed to be a good, honest man, though, and it wasn't difficult to see how concerned he was about his farm. He wants me and needs me on the farm. So I've decided that tomorrow I'll go up there and start work. It's more than I can comprehend. We hope that he'll be able to come home in a month or two, or I'll work with him at least for a part of the summer.

Please don't worry about me. I think I've made the right decision. I'll try to write again in a few days.

with love,
Liese

Dear Family,

Where can I begin? All of a sudden I'm in charge of a hundred sheep, a cow, calf and heifer, a horse, a dog, a farm, and a botanical garden! Johannes, in his words, gave me "full authority" here—all decisions are to be made by me and me alone.

Today is Whitsunday and the sun shone all day long from a crystal clear sky. Several families came up on the pretense of looking at the garden. Curious neighbors have been drifting over one by one to see what sort of girl it is who is crazy enough to work here alone. Both the Evangers and Ola Maeland's family (Ola is Johannes's brother-in law who drove me to Voss on Friday) visited this afternoon. They arrived at different times and, as they both came supplied with sandwiches and cakes, I made coffee twice and spent the afternoon picnicking with them in the garden.

It's getting a little easier to understand the language. The Maeland's have lent me their eleven-year-old daughter, Marta Johanne, who has been helping to orient me. She's an excellent language teacher, although we have quite a time trying to understand each other, and she gets a little irritated when I just can't understand what she says even after she's repeated something three or four times. It makes me feel stupid, but she's good company, and I enjoy having her here. She will stay until Tuesday.

In Norway there are two official languages—*Bokmål* and *Nynorsk*, but neither of them are actually spoken anywhere except perhaps in the theatre and on the radio and television. What people do speak are hundreds of different dialects, many of which are quite distinct from one another. *Bokmål* is nearly the same as Danish but *Nynorsk* has a somewhat different grammar and vocabulary. Unfortunately, it's a dialect of *Nynorsk* which is spoken here. From what I can gather, it's a very difficult and obscure one. It's called *Kvammamål*—Kvam is the name of this country and *mål* means language. Some of the dialect's peculiarities are that open o ("å") is pronounced "ao" and some words that normally end with an "a" sound are pronounced as if they ended with "o". It's fun to try talking like this, but I'm afraid that it's going to take many months before I'll be able to understand and speak properly. Right now I can pick up about a quarter of the conversation. There are not too many people around who speak *Bokmål*, though everyone understands it perfectly, so conversations are very often strained and frustrating. If I modify my Danish (all I have to do is to pronounce all the letters in the Danish words—Danes themselves only pronounce about half the letters), most of what I say is understood.

Today was my first whole day on the farm. I now have a better idea of the work routine. For at least another month, this will be my daily schedule: Rise at 6:30. Feed and water the animals in the barn. Then comes the fun—milking the cow. That's quite a job. The first time I tried, I got only a quarter cup of milk in the bucket after four minutes of squeezing that wore out my hand and arm muscles. This evening was my third attempt and it took me half an hour to milk half a gallon. I don't think that cow likes me. When the neighbor woman milks her, the milk comes right out, but not when I try. For the time being I will begin the milking and get as far as I can until Solveig, the neighbor, comes and finishes up for me. That way I can slowly build up my strength and technique. Have any of you ever seen a top-notch milk-maid at work? Solveig is astonishingly quick. She empties the cow and fills the bucket to the six-quart level in ten minutes. Her hands and forearms have muscles of iron.

After milking, I pour some of the milk into a bucket and give it to the calf, give Solveig some and the rest I take into the house and pour through a filter before taking it down to the cellar and putting it into the well for chilling. This house is built right over a rocky pool of crystal clear, icy cold water; the only "refrigerator" I've got. The milk buckets are hung onto hooks just above the spring and then float in the water.

After washing the buckets and filter, I go back to the barn and turn the heifer loose into the pasture. The cow gets tethered to a heavy iron stake that I must drive into the ground at a suitable site in the pasture. What usually happens, though, is that the stake hits a rock (I could market it as a rock-detector) and I have to drive it in several different places before I can sink it deep enough. Two or three times a day I move the stake and cow to a fresh grazing spot.

After doing all this, I go inside to eat breakfast. I've decided to use the mornings to do garden work and the afternoons to clean out the barn and to straighten up things in the house and out-buildings. It's awfully messy around here, as Johannes became ill just after the busy lambing time and didn't have a chance to do any "spring cleaning" in the barn. In the evening I repeat the morning's chores.

It's light here from about 2:30 a.m. to 10:00 p.m., so I feel as though I should be working all the time to take advantage of the light hours. The mountains, the air, the meadows—it's all so invigorating! I'm bursting with energy and feel like doing a hundred things at once.

There are many out-buildings on the farm. All are built of unfinished, hand-sawn, and in some cases hand-hewn wood. The only building that is painted is the red and white house. Everywhere I turn there are old wood and iron tools and utensils that are still in use: a manure cart, scythes, buckets, and a rake with wooden teeth, to name just a few.

In the cellar under the house, two wooden barrels hold what is left of last year's potatoes, and in three wooden tubs there are pig hams, shoulder and ribs curing in a brine solution. A few boxes of shrivelled apples are stored on a shelf and many wooden baskets, bowls and barrels are stacked along the walls.

Upon entering the house through the front door (the only door that leads to the outside), I step into the anteroom. From there I can either go up the stairs to one of three bedrooms, or open one of five doors that lead out of the anteroom and into the living room, kitchen, pantry, Johannes's room or a storage room.

There are several fascinating things in the pantry: a rack hung with huge chunks of sheep meat which have been salted and smoked, three large orange plastic buckets of plum jam, each covered with half an inch of blue-grey mold, a table-mounted cream separator, and dozens of other odds and ends that I can't identify. Johannes has decorated his living room with many of his mother's old tools, including a hand-painted chest, two spinning wheels, a cradle, wooden bowls and mugs and many other old wooden articles, which have surely been used here on the farm, but for what I can't figure out. The walls, floor, and ceiling of the room are of unfinished wood. A large, hand-woven blanket with an intricate Norwegian design hangs on one wall and Johannes's potted ferns adorn the table top, bureau, and window sills.

From the kitchen window I can see across the fjord to the glacier twenty-five miles away, flanked by many miles of snow-covered mountains. While eating breakfast at the kitchen table, I watch the pastures of Hovland full of ewes and lambs grazing contentedly. I can look downhill to several other farms and I can even see down to a tiny bit of the fjord itself. This is the end of the road and you'd have to hike dozens of miles into the mountains before reaching the next house or town to the north.

There's an electric stove here and hot and cold running water! I'd suspected there wouldn't be. The water is heated by electricity. Apart from the stove, lights, telephone, and hot water, there are no other "modern" conveniences—no dishwasher, washing machine (there is a wash-board), toilet, heating, or bathroom and not a single electrical appliance in the kitchen. For heating the house, there are four wood burning stoves, and the toilet is out in one of the sheep sheds. It consists of a bucket with a frame built around it. After use, I carry the contents of the bucket across the yard to dump them on the heap of cow and horse manure in the "manure cellar" by the big barn. The whole pile will later be spread out over the fields as fertilizer. Quite organic.

Begonia, the horse, is small, plump, and strong. Johannes has cut her tail short, which looks terrible, but apart from that, she's quite attractive. The Norwegian name for her breed is *fjording*—I don't think they are found in the States. She's a beige color with a darker stripe running down her back and she has dark eyes and ears. Ola Maeland showed me how to harness her and attach her to the cart and buggy today. In a few weeks I may ride to town in style. If you're not interested in a gait faster than a walk, Begonia does well as a riding horse, too. I believe that most of my farming neighbors are also dependent on their work horses.

My dog, Bella, is a little Norwegian *buhund*. That's another unique Norwegian breed. She's no larger than a cocker spaniel and she looks something like a small husky but for her creamy white color and shorter hair. She's very bright and well-trained and already seems to realize that I am the new master of the house, for she obeys me over others and follows me wherever I go.

Oh dear! It's already 11:30—way past my bed-time. Good night.

with love
Liese

Dear Family,

So, the first week has come to an end, and what a week it's been. Two days were rainy, freezing cold, and miserable but the rest of the time has been wonderful. It's going to be difficult to collect my thoughts to write down all that I've learned and done this week.

This farm and the two closest neighboring farms comprise what is called "Hovland." A little farther down the road is a cluster of six or seven farms called "Soldal." Everybody who lives at Hovland is named Hovland and nearly everyone in Soldal is named Soldal. This is because farmers used to take the name of the farm they lived on, not because everyone is inter-related (although some endogamy has occurred in these small communities over the last few hundred years). Every small cluster of farms (called a *grend*) has a name, as does every individual farm in the cluster. It's confusing to an outsider. People aren't commonly called by their official names, but after the farms where they come from e.g. "Trond" Ola, instead of Ola Soldal, or "Sjura" Solveig, instead of Solveig Hovland. This farm's name is "Andreas" after Johannes's father and Johannes is sometimes called "Andreas" Johannes. Often I can't figure out what someone's real name is.

Under Norwegian law the eldest son inherits the farm. If he won't have it, the next eldest gets it and so on down the line. If there are no sons, or if the sons won't have the farm, the daughters then have a chance to inherit. Hmmm— women's liberation should hear about this.* If a daughter did inherit the farm, she usually kept her maiden name under marrying so her children had the old family/farm name. Johannes's mother was the eldest of five sisters. She married a man named Andreas Haukås, but she kept the name Hovland. All of her children are named Hovland, too, I think. Since 1600 nearly everyone who has lived here has been named Hovland.

Oddly enough, the farmers of Hovland and Soldal are nearly all about the same age—between 50 and 65. Most of their children are scattered over Norway working or going to school. So nearly everyone who lives around here is older than 50 and farming. There are not many children in the families now, but the families of Johannes's generation all had many children. I've been told that 30 or 40 years ago there were 33 children on the three Hovland farms!

Everyone at Hovland and Soldal has grown up together and knows everything there is to know about each other. They don't ever seem to forget anything about anybody either. I've heard judgemental remarks made by one neighbor about another based on deeds committed 30, 40, or even 50 years ago. In conversation people talk about things that happened years ago as if they happened yesterday. Inger, my next-door neighbor, was telling me the other day about Johan-

*This law was changed in the mid-1970's. Now the eldest child, regardless of sex, has first inheritance rights.

162

nes's wife from the Faeroe Islands. It seems that the woman came to Hovland and stayed only a few months. From the gossipy tone Inger used, I assumed that this was recent news. But when I asked when she had left, Inger figured it was 25 years ago! I'd wager that a third of all conversation is about events long past. Maybe that's because there's not enough to talk about from daily life. In any case, I get the feeling that "the California girl living at Hovland" is giving my neighbors a lot to talk about now.

It's strange and somewhat uncomfortable to be plopped into such a tightly knit community and to be the only one who doesn't know a thing about anybody else. I am still not sure if some of the neighbors are brother and sister or husband and wife, or which house children belong to; I can't even remember (or pronounce) the names of most people! On the other hand, nobody knows anything about me, my family, or my past. I will be judged (*am* being judged) entirely on whatever actions I take here.

Solveig is the jolly, round country woman from down the road who took care of the animals when Johannes left and has been helping me milk. I love her. She talks and jokes with me all the time but I can never understand her. She is the epitome of the wise old peasant woman with much intuition and good-will. She has a way with animals—if she stands in the middle of the field and calls the sheep, they all come running to her. I'd thought that she must have a house swarming with children because she is so matronly, so I was surprised and even a bit disappointed to find that she is unmarried and lives with two unmarried brothers, Alv and Torgeir. They live on the first of the three Hovland farms. Their farm is called "Sjura," so the three of them are referred to as "Sjura Solveig," "Sjura Torgeir," and "Sjura Alv."

I can see only one house from here and it's about half a mile away. Although it's only a four minute walk to the front door of my nearest neighbors, Torkel and Inger, I can't see their house because there is a hill between us. Inger is from Bergen where they speak a dialect of *Bokmål* which is close to Danish so she is the one person I can understand. If several people are standing around talking, she translates from *Kvammamål* to *Bokmål* for me. Torkel, on the other hand, is impossible to understand. He speaks more dialectically than anyone I've heard, despite Inger's frequent reprimand to "speak Norwegian, Torkel!" Their cellar is stocked with barrels of Torkel's home-made wine (plum, pear, blueberry, and gooseberry), a bottle of which he often has on hand when I come for a visit. Two of their children still live at home, Tormod 14 and Arne, 12. They're very good looking, intelligent, and lively boys. When I first saw Arne I wasn't sure if he was a girl or a boy, for he's got long, blond hair and a round, almost angelic face. Though he's painfully shy, a few days ago he came up here by himself just to talk. I have a feeling that we're going to become pals this summer. I'm already beginning to feel at home at Torkel's and both he and Inger make me feel very welcome whenever I drop by ....

I had not intended to spend more than three months in Norway, but as the summer wore on it became apparent that Johannes would not be able to return home for many months. It was not a hard decision to make, to remain at Hovland, for by the end of August the allure of the Norwegian fjell *had permanently settled in my heart and I was in love with the farm and my good neighbors there. I remained through the long winter and well into the exuberant Norwegian spring, and I experienced the agonies of a farmer whose hayloft leaks and whose animals become ill during their long confinement, but I also learned to ski and to love the cold, dazzling winter* fjell *as well as its lush summer counterpart.*

After spring lambing I left Hovland and spent two months in California, then I returned to Norway to attend a small agriculture school in Nordfjord for a year. Along with 20 young farmers from all over the country, I learned a tremendous amount about all aspects of farming. After graduation I spent the summer working on the school farm and then worked two months on the coastal freighter sailing between Bergen and Kirkenes before finally returning home to California.

It is not always easy away from Norway, for the beauty of the Norwegian westlands still haunts me and the strong ties of friendships made there forever bind me to that land.

ACROSS THE SWAMP

Olav H. Hauge

Translated by Robert Bly

It is the roots from all the trees that have died
out here, that's how you can walk
safely over the soft places.
Roots like these keep their firmness, it's possible
they've lain here centuries.
And there are still some dark remains
of them under the moss.
They are still in the world and hold
you up so you can make it over.
And when you push out into the mountain lake, high
up, you feel how the memory
of that cold person
who drowned himself here once
helps to hold up your frail boat.
He, really crazy, trusted his life
to water and eternity.

HARVEST TIME

Olav H. Hauge

Translated by Robert Bly

These calm days of September with their sun.
It's time to harvest. There are still clumps
of cranberries in the woods, reddening rosehips
by the stone walls, hazel huts coming loose,
and clusters of black berries shine in the bushes,
thrushes look around for the last currants
and wasps fasten on to the sweetening plums.
I set the ladder aside at dusk, and hang
my basket up in the shed. The glaciers
all have a thin sprinkling of new snow. In bed
I hear the brisling fishermen start their motors
and go out. They'll pass the whole night
gliding over the fjord behind their powerful searchlights.

COUNTRY ROADS

Rolf Jacobsen

Translated by Robert Bly

A pale morning in June 4 AM
the country roads still greyish and moist
tunnelling endlessly through pines
a car had passed by on the dusty road
where an ant was out with his pine needle working
he was wandering around in the huge F of Fire-
  stone
that had been pressed into the sandy earth
for a hundred and twenty kilometers.
Fir needles are heavy.
Time after time he slipped back with his badly
  balanced
  load
and worked it up again
and skidded back again
travelling over the great and luminous Sahara
  lit by clouds.

GUARDIAN ANGEL

Rolf Jacobsen

Translated by Robert Bly

I am the bird that flutters against your window
    in the morning
and your closest friend, whom you can never
    know,
blossoms that light up for the blind.

I am the glacier shining over the woods, so pale,
and heavy voices from the cathedral tower.
The thought that suddenly hits you in the middle
    of the day
and makes you feel so fantastically happy.

I am the one you have loved for many years.
I walk beside you all day and look intently at
    you
and put my mouth against your heart
though you're not aware of it.

I am your third arm, and your second
shadow, the white one,
whom you cannot accept,
and who can never forget you.

SUNFLOWER

Rolf Jacobsen

Translated by Robert Bly

What sower walked over earth,
which hands sowed
our inward seeds of fire?
They went out from his fists like rainbow curves
to frozen earth, young loam, hot sand,
they will sleep there
greedily, and drink up our lives
and explode it into pieces
for the sake of a sunflower that you haven't seen
or a thistle head or a chrysanthemum.

Let the young rain of tears come.
Let the calm hands of grief come.
It's not all as evil as you think.

NIGHT BICYCLE

Ole Lokensgard

The world is thick with the soft gauze of fog.
In the still yellow cones of light beneath
The street lamps, the air holds its breath
For the padded passing of a sullen dog.
The wheels hiss as if the magic cog
Of earth spins below while I in stealth
Stand still and balanced in a wreath
Of cloud. A ghost moves by on its nightly jog.
The road extends, and time begins to lift
Again. Horns sound lost away in waves,
Sheep lost in the endless hummocks of the mist.
And in the dark, the island starts to drift
Over the unknown sailors' sodden graves
Into the broad atlantic wilderness.

THE MEMORY OF ISLANDS

Ole Lokensgard

"You seem to always end up on islands."
—Hjalmar "Lucky" Lokensgard

Iceland
Reykjavik, 1957
The frosted glass panes that covered the windows of the women's
Locker rooms at the pool house below
Austurbaejarskoli were pierced in two places
By BB's, tiny holes the size of a pupil,
Below which Maur would altruistically place himself
On all fours while Guthion, then Runar, then I
Would climb up and press our throbbing eyes,
Penetrating another world of steam and soft
Budding skin, looking for her, yes,
With the warm fog of the showers from hot springs
Bringing tears of joy and longing and deep tremors.

Walking the hot water pipeline enclosed in concrete
Across the lava-strewn hills on the edge of town,
We come to the river where adjacent pools, isolated,
Are clear down to infinite depth, clear down
To the bodies of immense salmon, majestic, aloof,
Poised in the remoteness of space, waiting, motionless.
We move to the edge of the river where the green lap
Of thick sod curls like a curb where we crawl
And lie flat, peering into a blur of reflections
Where dark shapes dart with undreamed speed,
Appearing and disappearing with the magic of medium.

And the mountains rise ragged against the scud
Of clouds, weather changing by the minute so
That no cloud can depress or keep down
The knowledge of sun. The mountains wink and beckon,

171

And we drag our skis behind us, breaking new
Steps into the crusted skin of the face steep
As faith, over the lip to the top where the seed
Of friends below dots the sheer snowscape
So far away that movements are barely
Discernible, dots shifting positions. And
The thought that we should go back before too long ...

Guam
Mangilao, 1966
She walked ahead in the darkness toward the sea,
And the coconut crabs scuttled in the thick-root clusters,
Stumbled in the stickiness of jungle and plumeria air.
The cloak of flora opened to brief sand,
Then luxuriant coral, flat, a carpet underfoot
On the edge of the lagoon, exposed with a thin skin
Of water at low tide. The moon's fingers slip
Into the folds of a wandering cloud. Now foot
Prints leap out, a phosphorescent trail across
The water. She leaves light where she touches
The earth, windows to another world inside.

Down the steep path through dense growth,
We find footing precarious. Through tennis shoes,
The pitted lava-lattice cuts with intricate blades
Rigid and brittle. The tanks hang heavy on our backs.
Fins flap against thighs. The lights probe,
And then there is sand, water! shuffling of valves
And masks, portable windows, and we are waterborne,
Carried with a light rip beyond the reef
Where a giant turtle wakes and changes us to Fokkers
Doing a slow chase, clinging briefly to the shell,
Searchlights, up and down, spectacle for parrotfish.

Four hundred feet straight down on a brilliant day,
The sea stretches out from the base of the cliff
As far as imagination rolled out like a rug,
And as the B-52's come and go overhead,
A great white shark swims, shifting its shoulders,
A mere guppy from this height, and yet more immense
For its inescapable presence, even at this pure distance,

For its obviousness: a slow probing white beast
Singular against the infinite blue-green sea,
The turquoise shallows blending into vague purples
Of a million accumulated years of coral growth ...

Nantucket Island
Nantucket, 1976
After dinner of bluefish broiled with mayonnaise,
Of light whitewine, newpotatoes, pale sweetcorn,
And the greenest of beans, we all go for a walk.
The town is settled in. The lights glow yellow
At the windows, contained, complete. Unwritten laws
Keep the shades open. This is the glimpse
Into lives, the presented arrangement of things of the past
To the continuous accompaniment of far-off music.
These are the stage sets, scenes or tableaux
Where the poses are struck, and there, from an upstairs loge,
An inconspicuous figure throws a rose to the night.

The impenetrable mirror of the water broke with rising
Wind that heeled us over and brought us hard
Against the tide that had dragged us out so steadily
Toward the channel, out the jetties for an hour.
Then we ran against the flow, strong, beating
Back toward mooring and the shore when suddenly
The water everywhere churned with bluefish feeding,
Surging, lunging in their frenzy, sending spray
Of minnows along the surface, trying to escape,
Electric in their panic, a shower of bright sparks,
And just as suddenly, then, they were gone from sight.

I lay on my back and watched the sky compose.
The stones are melting, the stones are melting the stones.
Light clouds furrowed into lava fields,
Foam enclosing, holding sensuous forms.
A blue salmon grew between the folds,
Then shrank away. A jet emerged and left
Ski tracks across an open stretch
And burrowed in again. The day wore on,
And the sun turned orange, burning the mounds
Into glowing coral, and then sank out of sight,
Having warmed the water for another night.

DOING AS THE WITCHES SAY

Robert Bly

Yes I am the son, new-born
in the Lutheran wastes
of Minnesota, like an eye!
Writhing on the bed,
newly woken from sleep,
I am a slave who hates
the sparks of the body.

Being content to hide
and have hurt feelings, I wake
in winter dark to row,
or scrub the closets
in a castle made of black
sticks, and I do
what the witches say.

ACKNOWLEDGEMENTS

Robert Bly: "Afternoon Sleep" and "Remembering in Oslo the Old Picture of the Magna Carta " are reprinted with the author's permission from *A Silence in the Snowy Fields* (Wesleyan University Press). "Finding an Old Ant Mansion" and "My Father's Wedding 1924" are reprinted with permission from *The Man in the Black Coat Turns* (Penguin Books). "My Father and Garth Morrison" is reprinted with permission from *Growing Up in Minnesota*, edited by Chester Anderson (University of Minnesota Press, 1976). The rest of the Bly material, including his translations of Olav H. Hauge, has not been published previously.

Ole A. Buslett: "A Funeral in Pioneer Times" is reprinted, with permission, from *Winchester Academy Ethnic Heritage Monograph*, number 4.

Knut Hamsun: "Zachaeus" is reprinted by permission from *Dakota Arts Quarterly*.

Jean Husby: "Springtime Rebellion" is reprinted, with permission, from *Plainswoman*.

Rolf Jacobsen: These poems, translated by Robert Bly, originally appeared in a volume of twenty Jacobsen poems published by the Seventies (now Eighties) Press.

Ole Lokensgard: These poems are reprinted, with permission, from *Temple Cat* and *The Nantucket Collection* published by Wright Impressions.

Rodney Nelson: "Karl Iverson" has been reprinted with permission of the author and *The South Dakota Review* (where it appeared in 1979).

Norman Reitan: These three stories are reprinted, with permission, from *Winchester Academy Round Table*, 1982-1983.

O. E. *Rölvaag*: "Cleng Pierson" is reprinted from *The American Magazine* (October 1929), with permission.

Johannes B. Wist: "When Bjornson Came to LaCrosse" is reprinted with the permission of the translator, Rodney Nelson, from *Dakota Arts Quarterly*.